SNOWDI

SNOWDEN'S BOX

Trust in the Age of Surveillance

By Jessica Bruder and Dale Maharidge

VERSO
London • New York

First published by Verso 2020
© Jessica Bruder, Dale Maharidge 2020

Parts of this book appeared originally under the same title in *Harper's Magazine*, May 2017

The moral rights of the authors have been asserted

1 3 5 7 9 10 8 6 4 2

Verso
UK: 6 Meard Street, London W1F 0EG
US: 20 Jay Street, Suite 1010, Brooklyn, NY 11201
versobooks.com

Verso is the imprint of New Left Books

ISBN-13: 978-1-78873-343-4
ISBN-13: 978-1-78873-346-5 (US EBK)
ISBN-13: 978-1-78873-345-8 (UK EBK)

British Library Cataloguing in Publication Data
A catalogue record for this book is available from the British Library

Library of Congress Cataloging-in-Publication Data

Names: Bruder, Jessica, author. | Maharidge, Dale, author.
Title: Snowden's box : trust in the age of surveillance / By Jessica Bruder
    and Dale Maharidge.
Description: First edition hardback. | London ; New York : Verso, 2020. |
    "Parts of this book appeared originally under the same title in Harper's
    Magazine, May 17, 2017"—T.p verso. | Includes bibliographical
    references and index.
Identifiers: LCCN 2019038432 | ISBN 9781788733434 (hardback) | ISBN
    9781788733465 (ebk) | ISBN 9781788733458 (ebk)
Subjects: LCSH: Snowden, Edward J., 1983– | Electronic surveillance—United
    States. | Confidential communications—United States. |
    Journalism—Political aspects—United States—History—21st century.
Classification: LCC JF1525.W45 B78 2020 | DDC 327.12730092 [B]—dc23
LC record available at https://lccn.loc.gov/2019038432

Typeset in Adobe Garamond by Hewer Text UK Ltd, Edinburgh
Printed and bound by CPI Group (UK) Ltd, Croydon CR0 4YY

For Max

Once you have the data local to you, copy it to more media in off-site locations so it is unlikely to be confiscated. Literally bury a backup copy in the woods, that sort of thing.
  — Edward L. Snowden, in an encrypted
  email to Laura Poitras, February 4, 2013

I've seen the nations rise and fall.
I've heard their stories, heard them all.
But love's the only engine of survival.
  — Leonard Cohen, "The Future"

Contents

FOREWORD

An Underground Railroad for Secrets

In the spring of 2013, an unauthorized trove of NSA files traveled nearly 5,000 miles in the care of the US Postal Service.

Postmarked May 10 at a former pineapple plantation village on the island of Oahu, the box of secrets soared east over the Pacific Ocean in a small flat-rate box, bearing a stamp for $5.80. It traversed the breadth of America before landing, unceremoniously, on the fourth floor of a nondescript walk-up apartment building in Brooklyn.

The sender had shipped the box via Priority Mail. He'd addressed it to a person he'd never met at a home he'd never seen. The recipient, in turn, knew nothing about him or the contents of the box. Her job was simple: carry it to a third person, who would ferry the package to its final destination.

At the time, to the best of the sender's knowledge, no one was paying attention.

By the first week of June, the whole world was watching. Secrets began streaming out of the box, onto the front pages of newspapers. They included evidence that the US government had created a massive surveillance apparatus and used it to spy on its own people. Intelligence officials blasted the unidentified source of the leaks and, warning of dire consequences, prepared to launch a criminal probe.

But before anyone could unmask him, the leaker revealed himself. The cover of the *Guardian* bore a giant yellow headline: "The Whistleblower." Below it appeared a photo of Edward Joseph Snowden. The twenty-nine-year-old had a patchy goatee and an earnest expression. He wore rectangular, semi-rimless Burberry eyeglasses — these would soon become iconic — with the left nose pad inexplicably missing. He identified himself as an NSA infrastructure analyst working for the defense contractor Booz Allen Hamilton.

The materials he'd taken, Snowden told reporters, revealed "an existential threat to democracy."

"I don't want to live in a world where there's no privacy and therefore no room for intellectual exploration and creativity," he added.

In the years that followed, Snowden's story would be told and retold, a ballad for our times. The saga unfolded in films, including Laura Poitras's Oscar-winning documentary *Citizenfour* and Oliver Stone's biopic *Snowden*, and in such books as *No Place to Hide* by Glenn Greenwald, Luke Harding's *The Snowden Files*, and, most recently, Snowden's own memoir, *Permanent Record*.

Missing from those chronicles so far has been a small but crucial episode — the journey of a plain cardboard box that passed through strangers' hands, setting the rest of the story in motion. In its absence grew a question: if the American government's surveillance was so mighty, so all-seeing, how did a motherlode of classified information get spirited away by mail, right under the watchers' noses?

The answer may be simpler than you think.

The story of Snowden's box is deeply human, somewhat messy, and more than a little weird. It's about a brief moment when strangers worked together to build an underground railroad for secrets — a high-stakes endeavor that relied, more than anything, on bonds of trust.

That's no small thing. We live in an era of suspicion, marked by an eroding faith in government, the media, and even each other. Social scientists have studied the decline of public confidence, quizzing Americans on the same set of topics over and over for nearly half a century as part of a long-term project called the General Social Survey. It includes this question:

> Generally speaking, would you say that most people can be trusted or that you can't be too careful in dealing with people?

Researchers ran the first round of the survey in 1972. At the time, nearly half of the people who responded said they trusted others. By the latest round in 2018 — two years after Donald Trump was elected president — the figure had dropped to less than a third.

That's scary news. Trust is the basis of all cooperative action in a free society. It's the feeling of fellowship that allows people to take risks and grow. It's also the underpinning of democracy. And it's fragile, easy to undermine. Massive domestic spying systems — like the one Snowden revealed — are corrosive to the kind of deep human connections that nourish trust and collaboration.

Consider East Germany, the most notorious surveillance state in modern history. Its secret police force — the *Ministerium für Staatssicherheit*, better known as the Stasi — was created in 1950. By the time it disbanded four decades later, the Stasi had grown to include some 86,000 full-time employees. If you add part-time and unofficial agents, the total number of people spying for the secret police had risen to more than half a million.

The population was saturated with snoops. Some estimates set the ratio at one informer to every six and a half citizens. Most major institutions — from universities to churches and political parties — were infiltrated. Neighbors snitched on neighbors, and mistrust was rampant. Even a member of the nation's Olympic bobsledding team, Harald Czudaj, confessed to spying on his fellow athletes. Years later, he recounted through tears that police had caught him driving drunk and blackmailed him into becoming an informer.

East Germany was an extreme case, but even in systems with fewer informants state surveillance frays the relationships between citizens. People grow wary, exhausted from the constant pressure. Eventually, they turn against each other.

"If we are gathering data on people all the time on the basis that they may do something wrong, this is promoting a view that, as citizens, we cannot be trusted," explained University of Sheffield sociology professor Clive Norris, testifying more than a decade ago before members of British Parliament. Today, the United Kingdom maintains one of the most extensive surveillance systems in the world.

The constant monitoring of a population, Norris and other scholars note, "fosters suspicion," undermines "cohesion and solidarity," and amounts to "a slow social suicide." In other words: paranoia will destroy you.

The Snowden affair created a groundswell of concern about how ordinary people are monitored by powerful entities, from governments to tech firms and other corporate interests. It sparked a public conversation on privacy, security, and freedom in the digital age, pushing our culture — at least for a moment — past the point of what the writer Cory Doctorow calls "peak indifference."

Before Snowden came on the scene, state-run surveillance rarely made it into mainstream American discourse. One of the rare exceptions came in 1993, when officials under the Clinton administration unveiled a device called the Clipper chip and proposed installing it in telephones nationwide. This cutting-edge microchip would encrypt users' communications, but it would also provide direct access for eavesdropping by intelligence and law enforcement agencies.

Privacy advocates, politicians, technologists, and civil libertarians were alarmed by the Orwellian plan. Together, they formed a motley opposition with members ranging from the ACLU to Rush Limbaugh.

"The precise object of their rage is the Clipper chip, officially known as the MYK-78 and not much bigger than a tooth," wrote journalist Steven Levy. "Just another tiny square of plastic covering a silicon thicket. A computer chip, from the outside indistinguishable from thousands of others. It seems improbable that this black Chiclet is the focal point of a battle that may determine the degree to which our civil liberties survive in the next century. But that is the shared belief . . . The Clipper chip has prompted what might be considered the first holy war of the information highway."

Polling showed that 80 percent of Americans didn't want their phones to be Clipper-chipped. So the White House mounted a bizarre public relations offensive, including a *WIRED* article by NSA chief counsel Stewart A. Baker titled "Don't Worry Be Happy: Why Clipper Is Good for You."

But that breezy, Bobby McFerrin–flavored headline wasn't enough to save the government's plan. Around the same time Baker's article came out, an AT&T Bell Laboratories researcher named Matthew Blaze announced a security flaw in the Clipper chip: hackers could use it to encrypt communications the government wouldn't be able to crack. The technology was sunk for good.

After that brief flare in public consciousness, dialogue about surveillance in America largely returned to the underground: a lively counterculture of cypherpunks, hackers, and digitally literate civil libertarians. It was far enough outside the mainstream that even Greenwald, who'd written for *Salon* and the *Guardian* about abuses of surveillance and went on to play a pivotal role in the NSA leaks, had given little thought to securing his own private communications.

When a mysterious person — using the handle "Cincinnatus" — pleaded with him to set up encrypted email, Greenwald blew off the request. "Despite my intentions, I never created the time to work on encryption," he later wrote. "It was simply that on my always too-long list of things to take care of, installing encryption technology at the behest of this unknown person never became pressing enough for me to stop other things and focus on it."

Cincinnatus was, of course, Snowden.

In early 2013, most journalists were like Greenwald. Protecting their email from prying eyes wasn't a priority. The general public was even less interested in such matters. In the immediate aftermath of the Snowden leaks, that changed. For many, privacy went from a curious abstraction to an immediate, tangible concern. Encryption got hip. At packed CryptoParties, grassroots privacy activists around the globe taught layfolk how to safeguard their online communications. By the time the television series *Mr. Robot* aired in 2015, the public was primed to immerse itself in a drama about a hacktivist collective. The show's first season averaged 1.39 million viewers an episode. Meanwhile, a handful of heavy-hitting tech giants followed consumers' interests — or at least their disposable income — and began touting privacy and security as integral features.

At the same time, all the talk of using technology to protect civil liberties may have worked to obscure some equally valuable truths. Chief among them: encryption is an important tool, but it's not everything. All meaningful communication and collaboration rely on a bedrock of trust:

people of good faith working together. The most advanced algorithms can't outpace that basic principle.

During a debate over secure messaging, Jon Evans, a TechCrunch columnist and software engineer, explained as much. "You always have to trust *somebody*. It's inevitable," he wrote. "Real security design is about navigating the compromises between usability and security, determining the sophistication and threat model of your users, deciding who you have to trust and who you can't afford to."

In essence, when it comes to trust, there is always a practical tradeoff to be made — unless you live on a desert island and you're a do-it-yourselfer who relies exclusively on homebrewed code, building proprietary smartphones out of coconuts and corresponding only with yourself. Faith in no one, after all, is a recipe for isolation.

Unfortunately, as Evans pointed out, we can't afford to trust others indiscriminately. Sometimes the figures who are most beholden to the public prove least worthy of its confidence.

That was true of James Clapper, who probably never imagined his tenure as US director of national intelligence would collide with one of the most significant leaks in national history. Three months before the first secrets spilled out of Snowden's box, Clapper was questioned by Senator Ron Wyden (D-OR) at an open congressional hearing.

Wyden's job, of course, meant he had a national security clearance. So it seems likely the senator already knew the answer when he asked Clapper if the NSA collected "any type of data at all on millions or hundreds of millions of Americans."

"No, sir," Clapper replied. He added: "Not wittingly."

That was a lie.

When his bad-faith testimony was exposed by Snowden's leaks, Clapper's first move was to deflect attention away from the lie. He assured Americans: a hunt was on for the dastardly individual who had stolen the government's secrets. "This is someone who for whatever reason, has chosen to violate a sacred trust for this country," he thundered.

That remark revealed either extreme hypocrisy or — even worse — the kind of cynicism that makes hypocrisy irrelevant. But the absurdity of making such a charge against the leaker, even with his own credibility in tatters, seemed lost on Clapper.

The intelligence chief would finally apologize for giving "clearly erroneous" information to Congress and the American people. Months later he would resign — his long career as a public servant derailed by deceit. But in the days following the first NSA leaks, contrition was not part of the script. Clapper focused on a single talking point: a traitor had betrayed America. In doing so, he underscored — over and over, as if immune to irony — the importance of upholding public trust.

During one especially revealing interview, NBC anchor Andrea Mitchell asked him how hard it was for intelligence officials to safeguard classified information. Clapper rattled off a litany of tools and protocols. He mentioned security clearances for federal workers and contractors, along with the spy-proof rooms known as SCIFs, or sensitive compartmented information facilities.

But even with the most sophisticated strategies the government could develop, keeping secrets was a "tough problem," Clapper admitted. After all, systems are only as reliable as the people who operate them.

"When it all boils down to it," he concluded, "it is all about personal trust."

Clapper may not have been trustworthy himself — but he was right to argue that everything comes down to trust.

That's why we're writing this book. The two of us are journalists, but, even more important, we're best friends. We believe in each other. And in an age of eroding trust, that was enough to make us part of the impromptu network that helped Snowden, a man neither of us has ever met — or even talked to — move his archive of state secrets.

More than six years have passed since those tense days. We're describing them now because we want to preserve these small moments for the sake of posterity. Above all, we hope that this story will help empower others — anyone who cares about an open society — to speak and act during a precarious moment in American history.

Meanwhile, the presidency of Donald Trump has brought new threats to democracy and transparency in government. Chelsea Manning, whose role in leaking US diplomatic cables made her an inspirational figure to Snowden, has been thrown back in jail, despite having received a pardon by President Barack Obama. WikiLeaks founder Julian Assange has been charged under the Espionage Act and now faces up to 175 years in jail. Meanwhile, Trump is pushing to restore the NSA's access to Americans' phone and text records, a practice that was exposed — and then derailed — by the Snowden revelations.

As we write this, a new whistleblower has emerged from

the intelligence community to reveal a startling abuse of presidential power: Trump pressuring Ukrainian president Volodymyr Zelensky to investigate the son of Democratic presidential candidate Joe Biden. The whistleblower alerted Congress of these actions through legally approved channels, an anonymous process that offers the full protection of federal law. Immediately Trump demanded to know the source's identity, deriding this person as something "close to a spy," and thundering about retribution.

In these times, it's easy to feel the creeping chill of suppression. So why would we want to tell the story of Snowden's box now? A book like this could make us vulnerable in the ongoing crackdown. Given how the Trump administration treats journalism as a conspiracy against the government, it could be used as road map to our indictment.

Privacy attorneys have made the argument that, by describing such sensitive moments in detail, writers risk "doing the government's work for them." But we feel differently. We believe that once people censor themselves and stop telling stories, the work of the government has already been done.

It's easy to believe that small things — individual actions and human relationships — don't make much of a difference in the face of an authoritarian regime. We disagree. We want this book to serve as a quiet testament to the power of trust, and why it's worth fighting for a culture where it can thrive.

Trust is the glue of the world, the difference between civilization and chaos. It's what lets people come together in any kind of cooperative action, from social movements to marriages and markets. When shared between members of a civic-minded community, trust is the one thing that can keep state power in check — unless, of course, we allow ourselves to be manipulated by fear and, in the silence that follows, grow apart from one another.

— Jessica Bruder and Dale Maharidge

Winter Nights

Dale Maharidge

It was a frigid winter, and the Manhattan loft was cold — very cold. Something was wrong with the gas line, and there was no heat. In a corner, surrounding the bed, sheets had been hung from cords to form a de facto tent with a small electric heater running inside. But the oddities didn't end there: when I talked to the woman who lived in the loft about her work, she made me take the battery out of my cellphone and stash the device in her refrigerator. People who have dated in New York City for any length of time believe that they've seen everything — this was something new.

That I was in her loft in the first place was strange enough. A year earlier, I was supposed to get married, but the engagement fell apart. After that, I was in no shape for a relationship and was in any case finishing two books on tight deadlines. I should have been too busy, then, to go to a party in Park Slope, Brooklyn, on a December evening in 2011. The host, Julian Rubinstein, had invited a group of his friends, many of whom were writers, musicians, editors, and documentary filmmakers. His email billed the event as a "fireside gathering," although when he attempted to get a blaze going in the hearth, the apartment filled with smoke. Through the haze, I noticed a striking woman with dark hair occasionally glancing my way.

"Who's that?" I asked Julian.

He introduced me to Laura Poitras. I was aware of her 2006 documentary, *My Country, My Country,* about an Iraqi physician running for office in his nation's first democratic election. Her current project, she told me, involved filming the massive data center the National Security Agency was building in Utah. Our conversation was intense, and I found myself wondering why somebody as sophisticated as Laura would be interested in me — at heart, I still felt like a blue-collar kid from Cleveland.

Suddenly, she announced it was late. "Want to share a cab?" she asked.

I shambled down two flights of stairs after Laura, and we hailed a taxi. We shook hands when we reached her stop, and I continued north. Two nights later, we met for drinks and exchanged a lot of passionate talk — about our work. When I saw her name in my email inbox the next morning, I clicked eagerly. Maybe she wanted to go out again? She briefly raised that as a possibility, but Laura had something more important in mind. Her message read:

If you want to set up a secure way to communicate (which I think every journalist should) the best method is IM with an OTR encryption. You'll need: a Jabber account, Pidgin IM client, and OTR plug-in.

Back then, this request — which would now strike many journalists as reasonable, albeit a bit extreme — sounded like gibberish. Why did I need encryption? I'd never done a story that would interest the NSA or any other federal agency. I initially blew off her advice, even as we got involved and began opening up about our projects. Which is how I came to be in that freezing loft, where Laura patiently explained why it made sense for me to put my phone in the fridge. I hadn't known that a refrigerator could block cellular signals. For that matter, I hadn't known that even when a cellphone has been switched off, federal agents can still use it to eavesdrop on conversations. Known as a "roving bug," this tactic dates back to at least 2003, when a judge authorized FBI agents to deploy it against John "Buster" Ardito, a high-ranking member of the Genovese crime family.

Laura's concerns, I soon realized, were anything but idle paranoia. She had been interrogated by US Customs and Border Patrol agents on more than forty occasions when traveling internationally. The harassment began in 2006, months after *My Country, My Country* was released. To create that film, Laura had spent eight months working alone in Iraq, chronicling the daily struggles of a doctor who was running a free clinic in Baghdad while also campaigning for a seat in the national assembly. On one particularly violent day, American soldiers spotted Laura filming from a rooftop. Their commander filed a report about her, speculating she'd known in advance about a fatal ambush and showed up to record it. That suggestion was grotesque, not to mention unfounded. Army investigators had "no credible evidence" to support it, a lawsuit revealed years later. Still, the report could have been enough to land her on a terrorist watchlist.

Whatever the government's suspicions, Laura had no way of knowing — or contesting — them. The experience was maddening. On some occasions agents detained her at the airport for more than three hours. Sometimes they temporarily confiscated and photocopied her notebooks. Once, they took away her computer. On April 6, 2012, after we had known each other for about four months, Laura was grilled at Newark Liberty International Airport. She was coming home from London, where she'd been filming WikiLeaks founder Julian Assange and his team for a documentary later titled *Risk*. As always, following her lawyer's instructions, she took notes. This time, a federal agent declared her pen was a potential weapon. He threatened to handcuff her if she kept using it. When she offered to write with crayons instead, he said no.

When I heard about what happened, I was on a reporting trip in the Rust Belt, en route home from the Monongahela Valley. I emailed her to commiserate: "Oh man, your re-entry sounds bad." She wrote back the next morning. By then, she'd recovered her sense of levity. "Oh yeah, it was really fun," she snarked. "Actually quite humorous, if it weren't so outrageous."

I drove through the night, reached Manhattan in the early morning hours, and slept. When I woke up, there was a new email from Laura. She'd pasted into it a message from the journalist Glenn Greenwald, whom she'd contacted about her troubles. He'd written:

You're a documentarian and journalist and the idea that you are routinely questioned, detained and have your stuff copied every time you re-enter the US is one of the true untold travesties — I will do everything possible to make sure it gets the attention it deserves.

Laura was reluctant to go on the record with Greenwald, even though she'd already reached out to him. She's an intensely private person. Besides, she didn't want the whole world to know she'd been filming the WikiLeaks crew. She had to protect her sources. "Do you [see] downsides in going public?" she asked me in an email.

"My instant reaction is yes, go public! Cockroaches are repelled by light," I wrote back. Hours later, I went to visit her in person and implored her to speak out.

Salon ran an article the next day under the headline "US Filmmaker Repeatedly Detained at Border." In it, Greenwald wrote:

> It's hard to overstate how oppressive it is for the US govern-ment to be able to target journalists, filmmakers and activ-ists and, without a shred of suspicion of wrongdoing, learn the most private and intimate details about them and their work . . . The ongoing, and escalating, treatment of Laura Poitras is a testament to how severe that abuse is.

At her request, Greenwald didn't write that Laura had been filming with Julian Assange and the WikiLeaks team. (In all likelihood, government intelligence agencies knew about this, which could explain why the border agents had been so aggressive.) After his story was published, the deten-tions stopped.

By one measure, Laura and I were a perfect match. We're both workaholics; we often debated who put in longer hours.

I used her as a sounding board for projects, and she did the same with me. In early August, she visited the solar-powered off-the-grid home I'd built in Northern California, over-looking the Pacific. The place is very remote, with the near-est utility lines some three miles away and the closest neigh-bor a half mile (as the spotted owl flies) across a canyon. We worked through the days and nights. I was finishing a book. Laura was editing *The Program,* a short documentary about William Binney, the NSA-veteran-turned-whistleblower. After a thirty-two-year career with the agency, Binney had retired in disgust following 9/11. That's when, as he explained in the film, officials began repurposing ThinThread, a social-graphing program he'd built for use overseas, to spy on ordinary Americans instead.

"This is something the KGB, the Stasi, or the Gestapo would have *loved* to have had about their populations," Binney soberly told the camera. "Just because we call ourselves a democracy doesn't mean we will stay that way. That's the real danger."

Though no charges were ever brought against Binney, a dozen rifle-toting FBI agents raided his home in 2007. One pointed a weapon at him as he stood naked in the shower.

After the *New York Times* published *The Program* in late August, Laura was ready to start editing her WikiLeaks documentary. This time, extra precautions would be neces-sary to protect her source material. Her detentions by border officials were still fresh in her mind, and the US government had opened a secret grand jury investigation into WikiLeaks two years earlier. So Laura relocated to Berlin.

Meanwhile, she was contracting out a major renovation of her New York loft. Having been a professional chef in the

Bay Area before she made her first film, *Flag Wars*, she was especially eager to have a working kitchen. Because I'd built and remodeled homes, she asked me for advice. I offered suggestions on such things as countertop materials (she chose concrete).

We remained connected, albeit with an ocean between us. Distance is hard on any two people who are involved. But ours was far from what most people typically consider a relationship. We were both under substantial stress with our work. That October, she came home after winning a MacArthur Fellowship. Her flat was still without heat, and it had a leaking bathroom pipe, which I tried (but failed) to fix. Then she flew back to Berlin.

I wouldn't see her for the rest of the year. But anytime I emailed, no matter the hour in Berlin — even at three or four in the morning — she answered promptly. This insomnia was chronicled in a journal she'd been keeping, which was later excerpted in *Astro Noise: A Survival Guide for Living under Total Surveillance*, published by the Whitney Museum of American Art.

On December 15, 2012, Laura wrote: "If only I could sleep I'd be happy in Berlin."

A month later, she noted in the journal: "Just received email from a potential source in the intelligence community. Is it a trap, is he crazy, or is this something real?"

Little more than a week after making that entry, Laura returned to the United States to shoot footage of the NSA's Utah Data Center, which was still under construction. According to the journalist James Bamford, the facility, which would begin operations two years later, had been designed as a repository for all forms of communication, including the complete contents of private emails, cellphone calls, and internet searches, as well as all types of personal data trails— parking receipts, travel itineraries, bookstore purchases, and other digital "pocket litter."

With these matters on her mind, Laura flew back to New York, where she told me how she'd been approached by a mysterious source who was eager to communicate with her. "Could it be a setup?" she asked. It could. Yet she chose to keep the channel open. We adopted a code for talking about the issue, pretending to discuss the ongoing renovation of her loft. On the last day of January, I invited Laura to dinner at my place. "I had a really good meeting with the contractor today," she wrote in an email that afternoon. "I look forward to updating you and getting your advice/feedback."

We talked about the source over dinner. Laura told me that this person wanted a physical address to use in case, as the source put it, "something happens to you or me." We speculated that perhaps the source wanted to send her a parcel. Hard copy? Data? It was unclear. Needless to say, the material couldn't go directly to Laura: her mail was surely being scrutinized. Nor could I receive it, because of our connection. She said we needed a third party, someone who wouldn't be on the NSA's radar.

"Do you know someone, a journalist, whom you absolutely trust?" she said. "Someone who won't ask any questions?"

"Sure," I responded. I immediately thought of the perfect person: my best friend, an author and accomplished journalist who also taught at Columbia. She had just moved, though. While I'd already visited her new place in

Brooklyn and knew what the building looked like, I didn't remember the exact address. I told Laura I would supply the location soon. Later, I mulled my options for getting the street number — what if, on account of my relationship with Laura, my phone or computer had been compromised? I didn't want to call my friend and ask her, on the off-chance that I'd been tapped, or pull up the address using an online search, in case there was malware on my laptop that could log my keystrokes. Instead, I went to Google Street View and dropped a tiny avatar on a busy road around the corner from where she lived, walked it to her building, and zoomed in on the number posted above her front door.

The next time Laura and I met, I gave her the Brooklyn address. I didn't confess how I'd gotten it, hoping my workaround hadn't somehow weakened our security. Since Laura was going back to Berlin and I wasn't yet using encryption, we spent some time refining our code to use on the phone and in emails. As we stood near my front door — she was on her way to the airport — I scrawled the following notes on a sheet of paper. (For what it's worth, the published excerpts from Laura's journal show that she transcribed the code a bit differently. Ours was not a system with exacting precision.)

— Architect = The unnamed source
— Architectural materials = The shipment
— First sink = The primary friend who would receive the architectural materials
— Other sink = A backup friend in California, in case the first couldn't do it

— Several countertops = Multiple packages
— The carpenter quit the job = Start over with a new plan
— The co-op board = The NSA or FBI (a tribute to the truculent nature of such boards in New York City)
— The co-op board is giving us a hard time = The NSA/FBI is on to us. Trouble!
— Renovation is taking longer than expected = No word from the source

Hours later, Laura emailed from the airport: "Thanks for checking in on the renovation work while I'm away. Hopefully it will be drama free, but that might be wishful thinking."

Meanwhile, Laura been corresponding with the source, trying to determine why this mysterious figure had reached out to her in particular. In an encrypted message that January, the person wrote:

> You asked why I picked you. I didn't. You did. Your pursuit of a dangerous truth drew the eyes of an apparatus that will never leave you. Your experience as a target of coercive intimidation should have very quickly cowed you into compliance, but that you have continued your work gives hope that your special lesson in authoritarianism did not take; that contacting you is worth the risk.

Laura arrived safely in Berlin, but her worries continued. What if the source was some kind of crackpot — or, worse yet, an undercover agent using her to target Assange?

WikiLeaks had already been named an enemy of the state by a 2008 US Army secret report, which also suggested a strategy to damage the organization's reputation by tricking it into publishing fake documents. (Ironically, that report was later leaked to — and published by — none other than WikiLeaks.)

Laura's source tried to reassure her he was legit, writing:

[Regarding] entrapment or insanity, I can address the first by making it clear I will ask nothing of you other than to review what I provide . . .

Were I mad, it would not matter — you will have verification of my bona fides when you . . . request comment from officials. As soon as it is clear to them that you have detailed knowledge of these topics, the reaction should provide all the proof you require.

Laura had also been wondering: What if the emails from the mysterious person suddenly stopped coming? Was there a backup plan? The source addressed that too, explaining:

The only reasons we will lose contact are my death or confinement, and I am putting contingencies for that in place.

I appreciate your caution and concern, but I already know how this will end for me and I accept the risk. I seek only enough room to operate until I can deliver to you the actual documents . . . If I have luck and you are careful for the duration of our period of operations, you

will have everything you need. I ask only that you
ensure this information makes it home to the American
public.

Still, Laura felt anxious. On February 9, she wrote in her
journal, "I still wonder if they are trying to entrap me . . .
My work might get shut down by the government."

Soon after making this entry, she gave me the go-ahead
to ask my friend about receiving the package. I wrote back
on February 12: "That first sink is definitely the cool one.
You always want to go with stainless steel. I hate porcelain."

A week later, Laura emailed: "Thanks for feedback re the
sink . . . The architect will be sending me links to view things
as we move forward. I'll let you know as things progress and
timing for doing a site visit. The co-op has been quiet. I hope
it stays that way."

There was occasional confusion as to whether we were
discussing her mystery source or the actual renovation,
which was still going on. In a few instances, I had to remind
myself: sometimes a countertop is just a countertop.

On March 15, Laura emailed, "Things are moving along
with the renovation. Still in the preliminary stages. I hope
things escalate soon." She was, in this case, definitely talking
about her source.

Before long, the source followed up with Laura, sending
her a pep talk of sorts. It read:

By understanding the mechanisms through which our
privacy is violated, we can win here. We can guarantee
for all people equal protection against unreasonable
search through universal laws, but only if the technical

community is willing to face the threat and commit to implementing over-engineered solutions. In the end, we must enforce a principle whereby the only way the powerful may enjoy privacy is when it is the same kind shared by the ordinary: one enforced by the laws of nature, rather than the policies of man.

I went back home to California for a few weeks, returning to New York on May 4. Still, nothing had come. Six days later, Laura wrote, "Quick update: My architect is sending some materials. Let me know when you get them."

I responded: "Will they arrive in the next day or two? My friend who is interested in those plans because of her own remodel is out of town."

My friend in Brooklyn had decamped to Los Angeles to report a magazine story. A few more email exchanges followed.

"I will know more when that friend gets home and settles in," I wrote to Laura. "I can't wait to hear about the design . . . hope it includes a window for lots of light!"

She replied: "I really hope he figured out a way around the co-op rules to do a window. Keep me posted — I'm really eager to see. If they are ready I'd like to get them so I can start reviewing Thursday. See you soon."

To which I responded: "Yes, windows are good. We can never have too many in our lives."

Jessica Bruder

Over the course of a decade and a half of friendship, Dale and I have shared all sorts of experiences. We've accidentally driven over a cow after midnight on the high plains of Colorado. We've cleared overgrown wilderness trails with chainsaws. We've extracted a rancher pinned against a tree by his own truck, and pruned branches from a thirty-year-old Douglas fir on Dale's California property using a shotgun. (They had been blocking his ocean view.)

Dale and I often jokingly refer to ourselves as a platonic married couple. I was confident that there was nothing he couldn't tell me. I was wrong.

In February 2013, I was hanging out at his apartment near the Columbia Journalism School, preparing to teach a class. Dale made a sudden request: could we put our cellphones in the refrigerator? At the time, that sounded nonsensical to me — like stashing our shoes in the broiler or our wallets in the microwave. We'd done stranger things, though. "Okay," I said.

His next question: would I be willing to receive a package in the mail for one of his friends? He didn't say whom the delivery was for or what it would contain. He just blurted something vague about "investigative journalism," following up quickly with "it could be nothing." I wouldn't be able to ask any questions, he added. Could I handle that?

"Sure," I said. "No problem."

The package, he continued, would be labeled "architectural materials." I should not open it. And we would never, ever speak about it over the phone — or even with our phones sitting nearby. Any mention of the shipment had to be in code.

"We'll call it the 'elk antlers,'" Dale said soberly. This was a reference to my dog Max's favorite chew treats. Elk shed their antlers each year, and apparently there's a small profit to be made by sawing the racks into bits and selling them to urban pet owners like me. Such deliveries arrived at my apartment regularly by mail.

I tried to keep a straight face. "So when it comes, I'll tell you, 'I've got the elk antlers.'"

"Exactly."

This sounds like a bad spy movie, I thought. But how do you tell that to someone you ran over a cow with? I agreed to help — even though Dale sounded paranoid to me — because that's what friends do. Frankly, it never even crossed my mind to turn him down. We retrieved our phones from the fridge. The day went back to normal.

For more than three months after that conversation, nothing happened. Before long I had forgotten about the whole thing, busy with my own writing and teaching.

Then, on May 14, I returned home to Brooklyn after spending a few days in Los Angeles for work. I climbed the stairs to the fourth-floor landing. In front of my door was a box.

That was weird. No one ever bothered to walk all the way up to the fourth floor. Packages usually arrived in a haphazard scatter in the foyer. Sometimes they didn't stick around for long. In recent months, quite a few boxes had disappeared in a spate of thefts. Their contents included vitamins, an LED tent lantern, a pair of earbuds, the book *To Save Everything, Click Here* by Evgeny Morozov, and a packet of Magic Grow sponge-capsule safari animals. That last item was to entertain my journalism students. In class we discussed the serendipitous nature of reporting — how small leads grow unpredictably into larger stories — and I mentioned the little gelatin caplets I'd played with as child, dropping them in water and marveling as their contents expanded to reveal the shapes of wild creatures.

Those items weren't the only things to go missing. Around the same time, my bicycle also got stolen. Someone nicked it from the boiler room in our basement. When I mentioned that to a neighbor, he told me several of his bikes had been taken too.

So it seemed remarkable that the thieves had turned up their noses at this new package. I knelt down to grab it. The words "architect mats encl'd" were scrawled in block letters on the front of the box. *How long has this been sitting here?* I wondered. After letting myself into the apartment, I took a closer look. Nothing about the package appeared unusual at first. It had been postmarked May 10 in Kunia, Hawaii, and sent via USPS Priority Mail. I shook the box gently, like a child guessing at the contents of a gift. Something inside made a clunking noise. Otherwise it gave up no secrets.

Then I noticed the return address:

B MANNING
94-1054 ELEU ST
WAIPAHU, HI 96797

What the fuck? I thought. *Is this a joke?* There was no way this package had come from the Army intelligence specialist turned whistleblower who'd used WikiLeaks to disseminate more than 250,000 classified diplomatic cables. At the time, Chelsea (then Bradley) Manning had languished for more than three years in military prison, awaiting a court-martial for the biggest security breach in American history.

Meanwhile, it was an unsettling moment to receive a mystery box from someone who might fancy himself a latter-day Manning. The Obama administration was zealously pursuing reporters who received classified information. The day before, news broke that the US Department of Justice had secretly seized records for more than twenty phone lines used by Associated Press journalists during a leak investigation. AP president and CEO Gary Pruitt wrote a protest letter to Attorney General Eric Holder, calling the move a "massive and unprecedented intrusion" into the news-gathering process.

Days later, the *Washington Post* revealed federal investigators had also seized personal email and phone records for Fox News Washington correspondent James Rosen, in connection with another leak probe. In one affidavit, an FBI agent referred to the journalist as "an aider, abettor and/or co-conspirator" — words that still give me the chills.

I called Dale to let him know the elk antlers had arrived, then tucked the box into a messenger bag and headed into Manhattan. When I arrived at Dale's apartment, I thrust the box into his hand.

"Check this out!" I gestured at the return address. "Your friend sure has a puckish sense of humor."

Dale looked it over. He was perplexed. I wondered what he knew — and what he didn't — about the package, but I'd promised not to ask questions. We let the matter rest and went out to dinner.

2.

The Brittle Summer

Your worst enemy, he reflected, was your own nervous system. At any moment the tension inside you was liable to translate itself into some visible symptom.

— George Orwell, *1984*, quoted
in Laura's Berlin journal

Laura's journal, various dates:

I am battling with my nervous system. It doesn't let me rest or sleep. Eye twitches, clenched throat, and now literally waiting to be raided . . .

I can hear the sound of my blood moving through my veins. Jesus, what the fuck is happening?

Jake says my friends will be targets and that I can't protect them . . . [he] said I needed to follow absolutely strict security. That I am a target they would do anything to compromise.

Dale

The rest of May wasn't measured in minutes, hours, or even days — rather, it was marked by steadily increasing levels of anxiety. The calendar says it was two weeks, but for me it was a single, excruciating unit of time. And if this was how I felt, what was Laura dealing with?

Laura arrived back in the United States on May 15. It was late at night, but she came straight to my apartment from the airport to get the box. Instead of opening it, she booked a hotel room using my computer (to avoid surveillance), then sped off in a taxi around two in the morning. For the next few days, she communicated with her source — who remained anonymous — from the hotel. The box contained data and instructions, and there was a growing sense that it involved something momentous. The source, Laura said, was treating the matter "a bit like a puzzle." There were multiple layers protecting the data, little of which she had seen.

As she absorbed all this, Laura tried to imagine what came next. How would it all go down? "I was thinking I was going to meet a source who then would be potentially arrested after. That was my read on what was going to unfold," she recalled later. "It was kind of going through my brain, like, 'Am I going to be renting a car?' All my scenarios were in the United States. Most were someplace in Maryland. I thought I might be taking a train to Baltimore."

To lessen the tension, we turned to gallows humor. One night, Laura and I met up for drinks and dinner with a friend and longtime collaborator of hers, the cinematographer Kirsten Johnson.

"When you get sent to Guantánamo, Dale and I will take turns using your steam shower," Kirsten said, alluding to Laura's renovation. We then brainstormed methods of communicating by clanging on bars if we all ended up imprisoned together. Things grew more ridiculous as the night wore on. "Thanks for making me laugh so hard," Laura wrote to both of us the next day. It was the last time I'd laugh for a while.

Soon after that, Laura insisted I begin communicating with her in a more secure manner. She gave me a USB flash drive loaded with The Amnesic Incognito Live System (Tails), a secure operating system bundled with a suite of privacy and encryption tools that funnels all of its users' internet traffic through the anonymous Tor network. Tails doesn't store any new data, making it practically impervious to malware. Whenever a session ends, any information it generated gets wiped away, leaving no digital traces. (Intriguingly, we'd learn later from leaked documents that the NSA considered Tails a "major" threat to intelligence gathering — a tool whose use could inflict a "loss/lack of insight to [the] majority of target communications.")

All I had to do was plug in the USB drive that Laura gave me, turn on my computer, and wait for the connection to be routed through proxy servers. There was a tiny yellow onion in the upper-right-hand corner of the screen — a homage to Tor's original name, The Onion Router — and when that icon turned green, it was safe to communicate.

I kept the flash drive, along with a sticky note listing both of our Jabber addresses, in a secret place.

For the next two weeks, Laura and I were in constant contact. The source, who remained nameless, finally revealed

the location to meet: Hong Kong. This raised the stakes considerably, and we spent much time speculating: was the source affiliated with the CIA or the NSA? He or she seemed to span agencies, Laura said. But that was just a suspicion on her part.

I was feeling in over my head. I'm more of a narrative or cultural journalist. I had been in my share of hairy situations when covering conflict overseas and even here in the United States. This, however, was a new dimension. I feigned steadiness when offering Laura advice, but my stomach was constantly churning.

In the early hours of May 21, when Tails refused to work on my computer, Laura fell back on email. At 4:49 a.m., she wrote: "Can you get in a taxi? I really need to talk."

I ran downstairs and flagged a cab; as the vehicle sped down Broadway, I peered out the rear window to make sure I wasn't being followed. When I arrived at her hotel room, Laura didn't speak. She pointed to my phone: the battery came out and the device went in the fridge. Then, eyes wide, she pointed to a file on the computer screen. It was NSA data — part of an extensive trove of documents. "It looks like the US government's covert intelligence 'black budget,'" she said.

When we reminisced about that day years later, it still shook her. "I remember seeing the black budget. It was the first document I opened," Laura recalled, starting to stammer. "Fuck! This is the kind of stuff —" She drew a deep breath and trailed off.

The black budget mapped out $52.6 billion in spending on top-secret projects for fiscal year 2013. Among other plans, it outlined what officials called "offensive cyber operations": an aggressive push by the NSA and CIA to hack foreign networks for the purpose of stealing information or committing sabotage.

After Laura showed me that document, she called up a letter stored in a file called README_FIRST. It was literary, even poetic — the words of a civic-minded person who'd clearly thought long and hard before deciding to make a startling sacrifice. This is, in part, what the source had written:

> Many will malign me for failing to engage in national relativism, to look away from [our] society's problems toward distant, external evils for which we hold neither authority nor responsibility, but citizenship carries with it a duty to first police one's government before seeking to correct others. Here, now, at home, we suffer a government that only grudgingly allows limited oversight, and refuses accountability when crimes are committed . . .

I understand that I will be made to suffer for my actions, and that the return of this information to the public marks my end. I will be satisfied if the federation of secret law, unequal pardon, and irresistible executive powers that rule the world that I love are revealed for even an instant. If you seek to help, join the open source community and fight to keep the spirit of the press alive and the internet free. I have been to the darkest corners of government, and what they fear is light.

The letter was signed "Edward Joseph Snowden." Along with the name appeared his social security number, CIA alias, and agency ID number.

Apart from learning Snowden's identity, Laura also knew she was more vulnerable than ever. Snowden had warned her about what he called a "single point of failure." If the federal government could stop the archive's release, he said, they would take whatever steps necessary to do so. That had a bad sound to it, I thought, as I pondered the stunning scope of the story and the dangers it posed to Laura in particular. To mitigate the risk, she made copies of what had come in the box and put them into the hands of other people she trusted.

Distributing leaked documents widely to avoid a single point of failure is not a new strategy. Daniel Ellsberg did the same with the Pentagon Papers. "For a year and a half my greatest fear had been that the FBI would swoop down and collect all my copies of the papers," Ellsberg wrote in his 2002 book, *Secrets: A Memoir of Vietnam and the Pentagon Papers*. A problem in that pre-digital age was sheer volume. He photocopied the documents furiously, filling boxes with duplicates. Then he had to find a place to safeguard them.

"One box went to my brother in New York," Ellsberg wrote. "Others went to friends' attics or basements in the area; almost none of them was told what was in the box, just that they were papers I needed stored."

Snowden, Laura said, had made it clear that he was no ordinary bureaucrat. Indeed, he insisted that this leak was bigger than the Pentagon Papers. Nothing in my career had prepared me for this moment, and, quite understandably, Laura was also feeling overwhelmed.

"I'm not a journalist!" she joked during a particularly stressful exchange.

"Yes, you are!" I replied.

"I'm just a chef!" she countered, referring to her previous career.

Laura asked me to be one of the keepers of the material. My profile as a journalist and a professor at an Ivy League school, she felt, would afford some protection. "Would you do that?"

"Sure."

She warned of the possibility of grave risk. She wanted to be certain I understood the danger, that I knew I could say no.

"This is what we do," I responded. "It's why we're journalists."

She muttered something about that being one of the reasons why she liked me. We embraced.

Laura still had misgivings about making the trip. What if she got detained again by the TSA? She ran through the scenario with Kirsten, who recalls feeling conflicted: the details seemed sketchy, yes, and they made her worry for Laura. But she also remembers thinking, "This is smart. It has an internal logic."

"One of the interesting things Laura and I do is we create a mirror for each other," she explained. "We're both risk-takers. Sometimes, she imagines the worst-case scenario, and I imagine the best-case scenario. But when we're with each other, we see things that we might not see if we were on our own. I have nowhere near her investigative capacity, but I really do think I am perceptive, psychologically."

Kirsten explained that she would have volunteered to take the trip with Laura, but two years earlier, she'd given birth to twins.

"I was ripped apart that I couldn't go," she said. "It was very clear to me that I had made a choice to be a parent and that I had an obligation, and it was immutable."

So Laura forged on. Now she faced her next challenge: convincing a journalist to join her on a trip to Hong Kong to meet a total stranger. The most likely candidate was Greenwald. They'd already met face-to-face in April when Greenwald was visiting New York and staying at a Marriott in Yonkers. Laura had them switch tables at the hotel restaurant twice, until she was satisfied they wouldn't be overheard, and had him take his cellphone back to his room. When Greenwald returned, she showed him a pair of emails she'd received from her source. She'd asked him to work on the story with her, and he'd agreed.

But now Greenwald was back home in Rio. That meant Laura had a trove of classified files on her hands — and no way to safely tell him about its contents.

"The problem was that he still didn't have encryption and would not travel without more information, which I would not provide without an encrypted channel to communicate on," Laura recalled. The situation was maddening.

Laura tried to help Greenwald set up encryption. In early May, she had Micah Lee, a technologist at the Freedom of the Press Foundation, send him a Tails USB drive with instructions via FedEx. But the package was held up in customs for ten days.

"I was desperate," she recalled. Going to get classified files in Hong Kong alone, without the support of another journalist or the legal protection of a major media outlet — that spelled trouble. "It would have pretty much guaranteed I would probably never be able to come back to the United States, if not be arrested," she said.

After all, she added, "I'm a lone wolf documentary film-maker already on the terrorist watch list, with the biggest national security leak in history. This is not a good combination."

Laura planned to film Snowden at this critical juncture, as he prepared to upend his life in the name of civil liberties. And Snowden was ready to take the hit. "My personal desire is that you paint the target directly on my back," he wrote to her. "No one, not even my most trusted confidant, is aware of my intentions and it would not be fair for them to fall under suspicion for my actions. You may be the only one who can prevent that and that is by immediately nailing me to the cross rather than trying to protect me as a source."

But it would all be for naught if the story wasn't disseminated effectively. Laura knew the material Snowden wanted to leak — documents revealing widespread abuse of power — would hit hardest as a series of written news reports. "It wasn't *just* a film," she explained. "It was a print story."

For the sake of safety and credibility, the print version would have to go through a large media organization, one with strong editorial and legal teams and a history of publishing ground-shaking investigative journalism.

Approaching the *New York Times*, however, was out of the question. Snowden didn't have confidence that the newspaper would have the guts to break the story. In an earlier message to Laura, he'd written, "I don't trust that the NYT will divulge the source document and company names until someone else does it first. Their reporters are fine, but their editors aren't what they used to be, and are far too accommodating of power."

He worried the editors would cave to government pressure, as they had nearly a decade before, when the *Times* spiked a story by James Risen and Eric Lichtblau about the NSA's warrantless spying on Americans. The scoop was scheduled to run right before the 2004 elections, but Executive Editor Bill Keller deferred to Bush administration officials, who claimed the revelations would damage national security. Frustrated, Risen included the material in his book *State of War: The Secret History of the CIA and the Bush Administration*. Aware that the book and its payload of revelations were coming in 2006, the *New York Times* was spurred in 2005 to finally publish a version of the story, which went on to win a Pulitzer Prize.

Snowden didn't want to see the *New York Times* sit on his disclosures for a year. To avoid getting tangled in the slow-moving bureaucracy of a large news organization, he'd decided to make direct contact with independent journalists who were passionate about exposing government overreach.

Meanwhile, Laura had separately approached Barton Gellman, a former *Washington Post* reporter who specialized in post-9/11 military and surveillance issues.

She'd proposed that they collaborate on a single article about the NSA's PRISM program. Snowden wanted to get that story out fast, though he knew the larger archive would take more time.

On May 16, Gellman had his first direct exchange with Snowden — who wouldn't divulge his identity and used the pseudonym "Verax," or Latin for truth-teller.

"I asked him, at the risk of estrangement, how he could justify exposing intelligence methods that might benefit US adversaries?" Gellman later recalled in the *Post*.

Snowden's reply was adamant. "Perhaps I am naive," he wrote, "but I believe that at this point in history, the greatest danger to our freedom and way of life comes from the reasonable fear of omniscient State powers kept in check by nothing more than policy documents."

Domestic surveillance, he added, is "such a direct threat to democratic governance that I have risked my life and family for it."

To find a news outlet for the PRISM story, Gellman contacted his former editor at the *Washington Post*, who was interested. Gellman and Laura traveled to Washington, DC, to meet the *Post*'s new executive editor, Marty Baron. Baron agreed to send Gellman and Laura to Hong Kong to interview the source. Laura returned to New York to pack. Then she got a call from Gellman saying he and the *Post* were pulling out of the Hong Kong plan but would move forward on the PRISM story.

"It was my decision. Marty said he'd back me either way," Gellman later recalled. "We were on a short-fuse deadline. Laura needed Snowden on film. I had to authenticate the PRISM document and report out the guts of the story. There was no way I could talk to sources over international phone lines, and no way to write the piece without the document in my hands.

"We all, including Snowden, agreed that some of the contents of those documents should not be published," he continued. "Carrying them to Hong Kong risked exposing the material directly to a US adversary. I decided to write the PRISM story first and travel to Snowden afterward. I was the first journalist to visit him in Moscow."

Meanwhile, Laura had other things to worry about. Obama's Department of Justice had been abusing its prosecutorial powers under the Espionage Act, which was passed during World War I and made it a crime for anyone to convey information that interfered with the war effort or promoted the interests of enemy nations.

The Espionage Act was meant to target spies — but Obama had turned the law against journalists and their whistle-blowing sources instead, invoking it more often than any of his predecessors.

Laura was terrified. She had a source who'd put his life in her hands and feared they were running out of time. She had to find someone who would travel with her.

She consulted with several lawyers including Ben Wizner, the director of the ACLU's Speech, Privacy, and Technology Project, who would go on to become Snowden's attorney.

Ben worried about the risks Laura faced. Her autonomy

and self-reliance, which had been so attractive to Snowden, were also liabilities. He looked back at the Pentagon Papers. "Daniel Ellsberg would not have gone to an independent documentary filmmaker. He went to Neil Sheehan at the *New York Times*," he later reflected. "My concern for her was that she is independent."

After Gellman and the *Post* pulled out of the Hong Kong trip, Laura and Ben met on a Saturday at a flatbread pizza restaurant in Tribeca. The place was empty. "That's when she dumped a ton of information on me, including that this is one of the most significant intelligence stories in a generation," he recalled.

Ben wracked his brain, trying to matchmake a media outlet for the story. Laura asked him if he knew anyone at the *New Yorker*. He did. Calling a writer at the magazine, he said that the story was potentially bigger than the Pentagon Papers. A meeting with David Remnick was arranged on the spot.

"I hugged Laura and put her into a taxi Saturday afternoon to meet with Remnick," Ben recalled.

Laura ended up meeting with him twice — first at his apartment and then at his office. She suggested that the *New Yorker* publish a profile of her source in Hong Kong, adding that it could be good fit for one of two journalists: Seymour Hersh or Jane Mayer. During their second meeting, Remnick asked for proof that the source was legitimate and for her to explain the story clearly and fully. She opened her air-gapped laptop and showed him a slide from the leaked archive. This, she later recalled, was the black budget.

Remnick's interest was piqued, but the significance of that single slide — and the position it might hold in a larger mosaic of leaked intelligence documents — was maddeningly cryptic. *Who was the source? What was the story?* It was evident that Laura hoped for the *New Yorker's* protection but, concerned about shielding her source and the materials in her possession, she was purposefully vague. Her anxiety was palpable.

Remnick wanted direct access to the trove of documents, which Laura would not provide. Without knowing more, he wasn't prepared to dispatch a reporter to Hong Kong on what could have been the mother of all wild goose chases. Frustrated, Laura shut her laptop and left.

As Laura scrambled to find a news organization that didn't balk at the Hong Kong plan, there was little for Snowden to do but wait.

"I left Ed hanging," she recalled. "There were a few days where he felt like he was completely alone. He felt everyone had turned their backs on him. I think he felt like sort of hung out, and felt betrayed. I regret that I put him in that position, but I did it because this was not a road I could go alone."

At this point, Laura asked if I would be willing to go with her. To be honest, I really didn't want to travel to Hong Kong. I was facing simultaneous deadlines to finish two new books, and one of them — about my father's post–World War II demons — had sapped a lot of my emotional energy. At the same time, I didn't feel like it was my place to go. This was Laura's project, and, to a lesser degree, Greenwald's.

But Greenwald still wasn't using the encryption tools she sent him, so Laura urged Snowden to contact Greenwald directly. She explained that all the unencrypted emails and phone calls among the lawyers at the *Post* — conversations that might fall into the wrong hands — could end up drawing a target on her back.

Snowden listened. He shared some of the classified documents with Greenwald. They discussed the situation. Then Greenwald convinced the *Guardian* to send him to Hong Kong.

"Glenn decided to pull the trigger and agreed to go," Ben recalled.

From Snowden's perspective, there were benefits to having two newspapers — the *Guardian* and the *Washington Post* — involved in the project. Snowden hadn't forgotten what happened to Risen at the *New York Times* in 2004.

"He didn't want there to be a single point of weakness, of failure, as he put it," Ben recalled. "Any one institution like the *Times* could be pressured. But if there's two, there's two things you worry about. One is government saber-rattling. And the other is your competitor publishing before you. So it was brilliant."

Soon all that remained was booking a flight to Hong Kong. But how to do that safely? Laura had used the same travel agent for several years, but they'd always communicated by phone. For the first time, she went to see him in person.

When she dropped in unannounced at his office — a small, spare room on the twelfth floor of a commercial building near Grand Central Station — her intensity was palpable.

"She was not nervous, but she was very hyper," the travel agent recounted. "Before that she never came to the office. It was a little surprising."

His clients often booked last-minute trips, but Laura seemed especially rushed. In the past, she had typically allowed him to show her three or four flight options, then held off a day or two before making a purchase. This time, there was no shopping around. She wanted to buy a one-way ticket on the spot. "Let's just finish this thing," he remembered her saying.

After the transaction was done, Laura told him not to email her a copy of the itinerary and confirmation details. Instead, she had him print it out and left with the hard copy. "That was a little weird," he recalled. But he figured the trip must be something personal — none of his business, really — and let it go.

On June 1, a Saturday, Laura and Greenwald shared a car to JFK International Airport. After passing through security, they headed for the gate and met Ewen MacAskill, a *Guardian* reporter the newspaper had insisted on adding to the team at the last minute. Together they boarded a sixteen-hour direct flight on Cathay Pacific to Hong Kong.

Jessica

In the days after I passed the box to Dale, he intimated that he'd been learning more about it. He told me nothing. "Watch the news," he said. "You'll know when the story hits."

On the evening of June 5, the *Guardian* published a top-secret court ruling. The US government had ordered Verizon to turn over millions of citizens' phone records "on an ongoing, daily basis." The newspaper was vague about the source of this classified information.

The story caught fire, dominating the next day's news. Progressives looked to President Barack Obama for an explanation. Six years earlier, while campaigning for the nation's highest office, the senator and former constitutional law professor had promised to end "the illegal wiretapping of American citizens." Obama had also denounced the excesses of the so-called war on terror, deriding what he called the Bush administration's "false choice, between the liberties we cherish and the security we provide."

But that man was gone. In his place, the sitting president scrambled to downplay the significance of these revelations, claiming they meant only "modest encroachments" on individual privacy. "You can't have 100 percent security and also then have 100 percent privacy and zero inconvenience," Obama said. "You know, we're going to have to make some choices as a society."

Civil libertarians reacted to the news with anger and astonishment.

"A pox on all the three houses of government," declared Anthony Romero of the ACLU. "On Congress, for legislating such powers, on the Foreign Intelligence Surveillance court for being such a paper tiger and rubber stamp, and on the Obama administration for not being true to its values."

Even one of the architects of the Patriot Act, a staunch conservative, was appalled. "I am extremely disturbed by what appears to be an overbroad interpretation of the Act," Representative F. James Sensenbrenner Jr. (R-WI) announced. "These reports are deeply concerning and raise questions about whether our constitutional rights are secure."

I absorbed the story, trying to process the enormity of it all. A national freakout was brewing.

I called Dale: "Is *that* it?"

"Yes."

"Shit." I felt light-headed. "Is that *all* of it?"

"No."

Over the next few days, more disclosures followed. The NSA had been collecting users' private communications from AOL, Apple, Facebook, Google, Microsoft, Yahoo, and other companies. Obama had told intelligence officials to make a list of possible foreign targets for American cyber-attacks. During a single thirty-day period, the NSA had harvested nearly 3 billion pieces of intelligence from US computer networks. And so on.

On June 9, the *Guardian* ran a short film by Laura Poitras. It showed Snowden answering questions posed by Greenwald.

One of the most striking aspects of the video was how placid it felt. The opening shot lingered over Causeway Bay in Hong Kong's Victoria Harbor, accompanied by the sound of a gently lapping tide. Then came Snowden's closeup. The whistleblower wore a gray collared shirt and sat in his room at the tony Mira Hotel in Kowloon, where he'd checked in under his actual name. His voice was patient and steady, almost eerily calm. It seemed he had contemplated this day for a long time, made his peace with it so deeply that, if asked, he'd be able to speak his own death sentence aloud dispassionately, as if reading someone else's news.

How long could this mood last? The moment felt like a short intermission — a breather between bookended struggles — with the process of orchestrating the leak now behind Snowden and the inevitable fallout still to come.

Only once in the video did Snowden's face break from a neutral expression. Greenwald asked him, "Have you given thought to what it is that the US government . . . might try to do to you?"

Snowden tried for a smile, gave a nervous grimace instead. Then he rattled off the bleak possibilities:

> I could be rendered by the CIA. I could have people come after me. Or any of the third-party partners. They work closely with a number of other nations. Or they could pay off the Triads. Any of their agents or assets. We've got a CIA station just up the road and the consulate here in Hong Kong, and I'm sure they're going to be very busy for the next week.

Knowing the risk of capture would follow him anywhere he went, Snowden concluded, "That's a fear I'll live under for the rest of my life, however long that happens to be."

This existential turn — Snowden's transition from enumerating grave risks to reflecting on mortality — mirrored one of the first things NSA whistleblower William Binney told Laura when she began to document him. "I want you to know I will never commit suicide," he said.

It also echoed a moment in *The Program*, Laura's short documentary on Binney, when a lawyer told him, "I don't understand why you're not afraid."

"Why should I be?" Binney countered.

"Because if what you're saying was possible, it would be revolutionary, and people would have a vested interest in preventing that from happening," the lawyer replied.

His answer was matter-of-fact. "I'm too old," he said. Binney paused, then repeated the words for emphasis. "I'm *too old*."

As all this unfolded, Dale was traveling. Though we were careful to avoid discussing the news by phone or online, it was clearly at the forefront of both of our minds. In one email, Dale explained he was working from his off-grid home in California, using his cellphone as an internet hotspot. "I write via Verizon (Spy-on-youzon?) from Humboldt," he quipped.

I waited until he was back in New York and we could meet in person. Then I raised the obvious question.

"All that stuff was in the box?"

"Yes."

"There must have been other boxes?"

"No."

And so Dale rewound through the past year, describing how he'd met Laura through our mutual friend Julian. I'd been dimly aware he was dating someone; now the whole story tumbled out.

The more details that emerged about the reach and sophistication of government surveillance, the more absurd our situation seemed. The gray-shirted guy in the video had sent some of the most sensitive intelligence information in the world to my home. It had traveled in plain sight through the US mail, then sat unguarded in my hallway, where it could have been pilfered as casually as all those other packages.

Thinking about that made my head spin. It also reflected what I consider to be one of the great lessons of adulthood:

that most of the institutions and endeavors we regard as ironclad — from parenting to politics — are actually held together with chewing gum and duct tape. Nothing truly works, at least not for long, or not in the way it's supposed to. This reality is terrifying, because it exposes the precariousness of the existing order. But it's also liberating, because it encourages the individual to act, to defy the ominous mythology of competence and control.

The only person I could talk to about all this was Dale. But he didn't seem to know the full extent of what was happening either. We puzzled over it together, unable to decide whether the plan had been ingenious or batshit crazy.

So what next? There was no way to predict how many more stories were coming or what they might reveal. I'd never been so close to something I knew so little about. It was bewildering, like having a front-row seat to a play performed in a language I didn't understand. Would I return home one day to find federal agents at my door? Should Dale and I be taking steps to protect ourselves?

Probably. I had no idea what reasonable precautions might look like, though, or whom it was safe to ask. I joked with Dale about a possible best-case scenario: years in the future, with this episode behind us, we'd look back and laugh. Then we'd coauthor an essay called "The Narcissism of Paranoia." Privately, I had also started wondering what the worst-case scenario would mean. I figured it was a good thing that I didn't have kids. I started thinking about who would take care of Max the dog if Dale and I got hauled away. Would the Powers That Be give a damn that I hadn't known what was coming in the mail until after the box left my hands? What did any of this mean, in a larger sense? I believe in civil liberties. The license our government took in spying on ordinary Americans was illegal — more important, it was unethical — and I'd held the proof of that in my hands.

Brooding over it all made me queasy. I worried because I didn't have a plan and, worse yet, was surely running out of time to make one. I worried that I was screwing up and might later regret how I'd used these long weeks of freedom. I even worried about *worrying* — and whether Dale and I were doing enough of it. "The only thing we have to fear is fear itself," Franklin D. Roosevelt said in the well-worn quote. But what if the opposite were true, and the only thing worth fearing was a lack of that visceral emotion? Fear, after all, can be a powerful motivator. Maybe more of it was just what we needed — something to lift the paralytic sense of dread and make our self-preservation instincts kick in.

My thoughts spiraled wider. By which I mean: I had species-level anxiety. What if our ability to adapt by normalizing insane circumstances — arguably the quality that has made human beings so successful — would ultimately prove our undoing?

The meta-worries pulsed in my brain. It grew hard to concentrate. Routine activities — grocery shopping, teaching classes, walking Max — felt surreal, as if I was acting out another person's life.

My thoughts hadn't been so hazy and dissociative since the weeks following September 11, 2001. From the window of my first New York apartment — a studio downtown on Christopher Street — I'd watched a plane hit the World Trade Center in a massive fireball that instantly killed hundreds and also seemed to incinerate what, moments earlier, I'd taken to be reality. For a long time afterwards, everything felt strange.

Mulling that history didn't help. Inaction was making me crazy. I wanted to do something — anything, really — to defend against the massing forces that were beyond my control. Months later, I devised a largely useless form of therapy. I'd been spending a lot of time on the roof of the apartment building where I lived. It had become a refuge in the days after I received the box, when Dale and I started building a garden up there: a pair of raised beds alongside a small greenhouse that managed to keep kale, bok choi, spinach, and romaine alive into the early winter. We called it the "veggie cathedral" — though in reality it looked more like a set piece from *Mad Max* — and modeled the structure off the larger greenhouses he'd built on his Humboldt property.

The roof was also home to a picnic table I'd crafted out of blue wooden sawhorses, the kind police use for crowd control. Originally I thought this was pretty funny, a piece of antiauthoritarian patio furniture. (Friends and I had called it the "pig-nic" table, part of a swords-to-plowshares effort to rebrand the NYPD as the New York Picnic Department.)

In the tense period following the Snowden leaks, however, my rooftop felt like less of a sanctuary. The table was too visible. Was it really a good time to stick it to the man? Every time a police helicopter buzzed overhead — a common occurrence near downtown Brooklyn — I'd get a jolt of anxiety. So in a novel form of self-care, I decided to cover the table with a weighted tarp. After that I felt a little better. But not much.

Dale

I flew to Sacramento the same day that Laura traveled to Hong Kong. That last night we met, I worried about going to California with a copy of the material.

"Should I check it in a bag or take it as carry-on?"

"Carry it," Laura said. She gave me a withering look: to her, that was a silly question.

"What about security?"

"They won't notice it."

"Do you think they know?"

"If they knew, none of this would be happening."

I still worried about being busted. I wanted to get home to my off-grid place and stash the item as fast as possible. But as I flew across the continent, with a copy of everything Snowden had sent us in an overhead bin,[*] a crown popped off one of my molars. I spent the next few days stranded in Sacramento, waiting to see a dentist.

Meanwhile, on June 6, the *Washington Post* broke its first Snowden story, which made me extremely anxious. Yet still I couldn't head up north. A man named Shane Miller had shot and killed his wife and two daughters, ages eight and five, then abandoned his truck on the beach road right below my house. Miller, who had spent much time in those coastal woods, was believed to be holed up somewhere in the canyons and ridges surrounding my property. A manhunt was on. So I delayed my return by a few more

---

[*] When we fact-checked a draft of this book with Laura, she wrote Dale an eye-rolling note on this less-than-strategic decision. "Seriously?" she wrote. "The overhead bin? Oy."

days, until I couldn't take it anymore — I needed to hide the material now.

An hour north of Sacramento on Interstate 5, I noticed a blue truck right behind me; it kept the same distance whether I sped up or slowed down. I turned off on California 20 towards the coast. The truck disappeared. I stopped for coffee. Miles later, the blue truck was once again behind me, and then it was lost from sight, and then it reappeared on US 101 before vanishing for good. Jesus! I flashed back to the year 1984, when I had been documenting the religious underground that brought Salvadoran refugees north to escape the country's civil war. For various reasons, I ended up smuggling a family with a toddler through northern Mexico, driving them in a panel wagon around a Mexican government checkpoint on dirt roads that vanished when we hit the base of the Sierra Madre, then heading north over rough terrain between the cacti and other desert flora.

I digress for a purpose. In El Salvador, government agents followed us openly. Ditto for Mexico. They wanted us to know we were being watched: it was a form of intimidation. Was this a similar tactic? Or was I simply being paranoid? In any case, the morning after I arrived home, a black helicopter was hovering over my land. Was it local cops looking for Miller, or the feds watching me? The previous night, I had sealed the Snowden material and placed it beneath an old outhouse, abandoned since I'd installed a septic system, inside a fifty-five-gallon barrel of old shit. It seemed way too obvious a hiding place. Eventually, the material ended eighty feet up an old-growth Douglas fir in my forest.

Through Laura, Snowden had instructed me to burn the original shipping box he'd sent from Hawaii to Brooklyn.

She asked me to shoot video of the conflagration. I prepared to follow her instructions, but something stopped me — I couldn't bring myself to set the thing on fire.

I spent the next two weeks barricaded in my house with the shutters drawn. I had a loaded shotgun at the ready for Miller, but I was afraid of going outside with the weapon: that could be a fatal move if the feds showed up for the Snowden material. Eventually, though, I had to emerge to split log rounds for the woodstove, the building's sole source of heat on that chilly coast. It was a Hobson's choice. When I went to the woodpile, I carried the gun.

Jessica

Through the rest of June, disclosures from the NSA archive continued. Snowden was all over the news. Frustrated by their inability to stem the growing torrent of leaks, federal officials charged him with espionage and asked authorities in Hong Kong to arrest him.

But the extradition request contained a critical error: Snowden's middle name. The US government had bungled it, writing "James" instead of "Joseph."

Snowden was allowed to depart. He boarded an Aeroflot plane bound for Moscow with Sarah Harrison, an editor for WikiLeaks. She'd orchestrated his departure and would spend the next forty days with him holed up in Sheremetyevo Airport, as they continued to make his case for asylum.

Meanwhile, life in Brooklyn was quiet. My worries about safety had started to abate.

Then July brought a new and startling revelation. The US Postal Service had been photographing and logging every single piece of mail it processed: 160 billion items in 2012 alone. The practice was exposed by the *New York Times,* which declared that "postal mail is subject to the same kind of scrutiny that the National Security Agency has given to telephone calls and e-mail."

It had seemed like good old-fashioned mail was one of the final frontiers of privacy — an analog holdout in a world where digital communications were increasingly insecure. Clearly the method had limitations. Still, if used judiciously, it remained one of the safer ways to send data. Several months after the *Times* scoop, Jimmy Carter noted that he used snail mail as a sort of low-tech counter-surveillance measure. "When I want to communicate with a foreign leader privately," he told *Meet the Press*, "I type or write a letter myself, put it in the post office, and mail it." Three years later, *New York Times* reporter Susanne Craig would find a surprise in her third-floor mailbox: then–presidential candidate Donald Trump's tax returns. This prompted her to remind the newspaper's readers that "especially nowadays, when people are worried that anything sent by email will leave forensic fingerprints, 'snail mail' is a great way to communicate with us anonymously."

At some point after Snowden's box arrived, I began to wonder about its backstory. What's the best way to keep sensitive information safe, while camouflaging your identity? Had Snowden actually sent the package himself — or did he have a trusted friend drop it at the post office? Had he done anything to keep authorities from connecting the package to him?

Something nagged at me. I went to my laptop to consult a photograph of the box, which I'd taken before delivering it to Dale. I reviewed the return address again:

B MANNING
94-1054 ELEU ST
WAIPAHU, HI 96797

Shortly after Snowden unmasked himself, the media had descended on Waipahu, Hawaii, where he had rented a home about seven miles south of the NSA's Kunia Regional Security Operations Center, his former workplace. In one of the news reports I saw that he lived at 94-1044 Eleu Street. Snowden, it would appear, had addressed the package himself. And he had done it while flipping the bird to the US Postal Service: using the pseudonym B. Manning and changing only a single digit of his actual home address.

This amazed me. Why bother taking any precautions at all if you're going to play a joke like that? What's more, he had written my full name and address on the box: information I had volunteered because I trusted Dale. Now anyone who wanted to track packages sent from Waipahu to New York in the month of May — how many could there have been, really? — would easily identify the shipment. Someday, I vowed, I'd ask Snowden why he had done that. Why not ship the box under a random name, from some other town? For now, I just hoped it wouldn't jeopardize the security of the operation or get me burned.

There was something else on the box I hadn't noticed before: a bar code with a tracking number. Perversely, I felt tempted to plug it into the USPS website to learn exactly when the package had been delivered, how long it had sat unattended in my hallway. But I was too nervous. It already seemed miraculous that the box had traveled so many miles without incident in the care of a federal agency. Using a public government resource to learn more about its journey — mostly for the sake of my own curiosity — seemed like the definition of "pushing your luck." I decided against it.

That was a good choice. A bit of research would later turn up something that simply hadn't occurred to me: the USPS logs the IP addresses of all customers who track mail on its website. In 2013, a Massachusetts drug dealer was busted after tracking shipments of methylone — similar to MDMA — that he had ordered from China. His digital footprints led investigators right to him. After pleading guilty, he was sentenced to more than eight years in prison.

It was probably for the best that I didn't know that in the moment, since it would have just made me more nervous. Like Dale, I felt utterly unprepared for anything that might happen. Being a journalist was no help — I couldn't talk about anything that was going on, and, besides, much of my reporting focused on subcultures. I had written a book about Burning Man and was now in the early stages of researching a new one, *Nomadland*, about older Americans who'd traded traditional homes for vans and RVs, becoming itinerant workers to navigate an increasingly polarized economy.

The whole situation continued to make me uneasy. Meanwhile, Snowden had fled from Hong Kong and was stranded in Moscow, where he was seeking asylum. Greenwald was in Rio de Janeiro, where he lived. Laura had decamped once again to Berlin.

The next time I spoke to Dale, I had a new question.

"Are we the only people who had anything to do with this who haven't left the country?"

"I don't know," he said.

Maybe there were others, we speculated: additional bit players in the affair, living in separate silos of paranoia. There was no way to tell.

3.

The Players

Around the time the leaks began, we started calling Laura "the Chef," a tongue-in-cheek nickname that referred to her earlier profession. We learned much later that the title was apt in another way. As the Snowden story unfolded, she had masterfully orchestrated the various players required to transmit and safeguard his information, as if working with ingredients in a recipe.

"I'm very proud of my network," she told us following a dinner together years after the operation. "One thing I have a good sense of is who to trust."

Part of her strategy, she explained, was spreading the information beyond her immediate circle. She chose people whose work seemed to align with hers. That made her feel more comfortable.

But she knew there was a downside to disseminating the material, even if everyone in her network was trustworthy. It meant the recipients would be vulnerable to risks they couldn't even begin to fathom.

"Yeah, let's face it: it was exposing a lot of people that I care about," Laura reflected. "I had no clue of the scale or scope. I just had no clue. If I'd had a clue, I don't know . . . I would probably have been a little more scared than I already was. Which was pretty terrified."

As far as we know, there were five of us in that initial network. In other words, beyond the two of us, three people we didn't know had received duplicates of the NSA leaks before Laura traveled to Hong Kong. Snowden had viewed his meeting with Laura as extremely risky, she later explained. "To mitigate the risk," she said, "there had to be a way of making sure that if we were both arrested, the story didn't stop."

Of the three people who got copies of the archive, two asked to remain private. The third was Trevor Timm, a lawyer, journalist, and activist who is the executive director of the nonprofit Freedom of the Press Foundation, whose board members include Laura and Greenwald.

Trevor received a nondescript package through the US Postal Service in the spring of 2013, bearing the return address of someone he knew.

"Nobody said a package was coming for me," he said, recalling his experience three years later during an interview in San Francisco. The contents included a note from Laura, which explained that she and Glenn Greenwald were working on a big story and asked if Trevor could hold on to the enclosed material. Taking an ominous tone, the message added: "Don't give it to anybody except Glenn, and only if Glenn asks for it in person."

Trevor put the package in a safe place. At the time, he was overwhelmed with work, and he soon forgot about the whole business—until the *Guardian* published its first story from the Snowden archive.

Trevor was, as he later recalled, "shoulder deep in the Manning trial on June 5th. Then it suddenly dawned on me. 'Oh, shit. *This* is the story.'" Soon after the story broke, he spoke on the phone with Greenwald, who indicated that there were many more to come.

Other people played key roles in the operation, even if they hadn't received copies of the material. One of them was Kirsten Johnson, the filmmaker. In the early days of the Snowden saga, Kirsten was among Laura's only confidants. She had collaborated with Laura since 2009 on documentaries exploring the reach of American surveillance, though her concerns about the abuse of state power began well before that.

"My first real encounter with a surveillance state was Sudan, when I went to film for *Darfur Now*," Kirsten recalled, referring to the 2007 documentary on the genocide in the western Sudan. "This was very low-tech surveillance. To make the film, you had to check in with this ministry. Every morning they would say to us, 'So why were you at this corner? Why did you stop and film something that corner? Why were we filming that house?' Twelve people over the course of the day had gone to the government and said they saw you standing on 'X' corner."

Kirsten and the film crew were assisted by relief workers and advocates. She said their emails were being read by the government. She knew that every move she made was being monitored.

"Filming there is completely intimidating," she recalled. "It's not even technology. It's just creating a climate in which people know they're being watched."

A few years later, Kirsten was shooting footage for Laura's 2010 documentary, *The Oath*. The film followed two men who had been close with Osama bin Laden: his former bodyguard, Abu Jandal, who was working as a taxi driver in San'aa, Yemen, and his chauffeur, Salim Hamdan, locked away in the US military prison at Guantánamo Bay Naval Base in Cuba.

The controls on what and how Kirsten could film at Guantánamo were severe. They made the kind of surveillance she'd previously associated with working abroad feel chillingly close, reshaping her perceptions of how government power is exercised in America. "It was now my own country — my own relationship to my own country," she mused.

Despite a long career working in conflict zones and covering trauma, Kirsten said she'd never experienced the sort of hyper-real, "dialed up" intensity she felt while advising Laura in the spring of 2013.

"I don't know if it was possible to document the feeling that we had. I'm someone who has hubristic desires, like I have some sort of narcissistic fantasy," Kirsten said, adding that many journalists crave a similar feeling — that their work is at the apex of what the world needs to know. "But then I'm really skeptical of it, I'm just like, 'Puh-lease, you may feel like you're in the center of history, but that's a joke.'"

As the mysterious source called Citizenfour began to tell Laura more about the material he planned to leak, it dawned on Kirsten that, this time, they truly *were* in the middle of a world-shaping story. How surreal that was hit her especially hard during one visit from Laura.

"I remember us going down into the laundry room at my apartment building, sitting and talking about whoever Citizenfour was, with the dryers going," Kirsten recalled. "I was just thinking, 'No one will ever believe this.' How is this possible, that we're in my laundry room to have the sound of the dryers cover what we're saying?"

Kirsten was on hand with her camera when Laura found a creative way to back up some files from the Snowden archive. At the time, Laura was still renovating her apartment. Kirsten filmed her dropping a USB drive into a mixer tumbling the wet cement that would become her new countertops. This footage became a vignette in Kirsten's film *Cameraperson* and also appeared in *Astro Noise*, Laura's show at the Whitney Museum of Art.

Another key player in the early stages of the leak was Micah Lee, a computer security engineer and open source software developer who lived in a Berkeley cottage with his wife and two cats. From childhood on, he'd pursued the interests that would make him indispensable to the Snowden operation.

Born in 1985, Micah grew up mostly in Asheville, North Carolina, where his dad ran a computer consulting business. His older brother was a programmer, and Micah was, in his own words, "a really big computer nerd" in high school. By age fifteen, he'd taught himself to code in C++ so he could write video games.

After Micah left home for Boston University in 2005, he discovered politics and a new passion: protesting the Iraq War. A year later, he dropped out to dedicate himself to activism. Scrambling for a way to support himself, Micah began freelancing as a web designer — an area in which he excelled, despite his lack of formal training. He also realized that the same computer skills he'd been using to pay the bills could bolster his work as an activist. He began volunteering in web development for Earth First!, the radical environmental group.

In 2009, Micah moved to San Francisco. After six months stringing together odd jobs from Craigslist, he got hired full-time at Radical Designs, a worker-owned cooperative in Oakland that builds websites for social justice organizations. Roughly two years after that, Micah landed his dream job: doing web development for the Electronic Frontier Foundation, a nonprofit digital rights advocacy group.

Micah's infatuation with EFF had begun long before he landed in California. It dated to at least 2006, when an AT&T communications technician named Mark Klein brought proof to EFF that his employer was helping federal agents monitor Americans' private conversations. EFF took up the whistleblower's cause, suing the NSA. That display of courage inspired Micah.

"Klein was in San Francisco at the AT&T Folsom Street office, which is one of the major exchanges for the internet on the West Coast," Micah recalled. "A lot of the internet travels through that building. I heard this story from people at EFF—one day, someone just showed up at their office, like knocked on the door. He was really nervous and sweaty and said that he had a bunch of documents to show them."

Now Micah had a chance to help his heroes. Before he was hired, EFF had used an outside firm to manage its membership database. But that practice made sensitive information unnecessarily vulnerable. What would happen if authorities approached the firm, demanding EFF members' identities or other private details?

"They wanted to stop using a third-party company and start hosting all of their data in-house, so that they would get any subpoenas for their membership directly," he explained.

Micah handled that transition. He also created a donation portal for EFF, building all the fund-raising pages from scratch because, in his words, "The open-source tools that were available were crap."

Micah loved his new job. Apart from enabling him to serve a cause he cared about, the work brought him into close contact with smart, like-minded people. They included Trevor, who arrived at EFF seven months after Micah and went on in 2012 to cofound the Freedom of the Press Foundation, whose early projects included helping WikiLeaks raise funds after its PayPal, MasterCard, and Visa accounts were frozen in what EFF called an "economic blockade." Trevor hired Micah to build the foundation's online presence and create a crowdfunding platform.

Micah was tireless, digging into these new assignments alongside his full-time job at EFF. Before long, he'd completed the Freedom of the Press Foundation's first website. One of the pages had short biographies of personnel — mostly board members, including Laura and Greenwald, along with other well-known civil liberties champions such as the Pentagon Papers whistleblower Daniel Ellsberg; John Perry Barlow, the former Grateful Dead lyricist who helped create EFF; and Xeni Jardin, a founder and editor of the blog *Boing Boing*.

As the organization's lone staff member, Micah appeared at the bottom of the page. Though possibly the least-known figure on that roster of boldfaced names, he stood out. His portrait, shot in profile, showed a young man with a scraggly beard, gazing through black-framed, rectangular glasses away from the camera, out into the distance. And unlike any of the others, Micah's biography ended in a strange garble — this series of forty letters and numerals:

5C17 6163 61BD 9F92 422A C08B B4D2 5A1E 9999 9697

The text wasn't as random as it appeared. It was an invitation, aimed at any reader who wanted to send Micah a secret message. Savvy readers would recognize it as a "fingerprint": a short verification code used in a system called public key encryption.

Anyone who used encryption would know what to do next to contact Micah. The first step was searching for him in an online directory of encryption keys. Micah's entry there would include his name and email address, along with his public key — a unique code, thousands of digits long — and a shorter, forty-digit code: his fingerprint.

But anyone can create an entry like that. What if an imposter was pretending to be Micah Lee? To avoid that danger, smart crypto users would insist on verifying they had found the real Micah. To do that, they could compare the two sets of fingerprints — one from the public key server, the other from the Freedom of the Press website. If the fingerprints matched, it was reasonably safe to go ahead and write to Micah using his public key and an OpenPGP-compatible encryption program, such as PGP (Pretty Good Privacy) or GPG (Gnu Privacy Guard), free software that uses the same open-source standard as PGP. The software could translate text into messages only Micah could decrypt, using a private key known solely to him.

To anyone else, the encrypted email would look like an inscrutable string of nonsense, something like this:

-----BEGIN PGP MESSAGE-----Comment: GPGTools - https://gpgtools.org

HQGMAzspJ5DWdx8MAQv/UXtFAJDKNgtE J0YUPb3Jt2xVZZYxarIH+4TXlx1dY KAFQlN8NSgjGC3CYBsHdgNE2xbvt1H- J71PrLeXy8KYqxKRR9USM9z7ePq7IIZgkpfvLo/ vKn34WpYjIJpI4hUWK4mH+8Af9pRxRjL9 MNYUL1e5Nm9pnfm1JQF6unTOSgwOXeeshPZ- KIwwBQC6/LPLb8kdD H4Fl3Gz6Aaf+NtVUjYOLzCWWQ6gA8dQNd6e- ISs7exrOxkJWwIT6DgMvjNlnR0gKhBxEt 0M4PziJsOfeCF2t2pgb 0L36Rqvtou5lg5YEsqlZd4KRa7QLGAZSuA 8AGB5rPLxww4TJteNTLHuZpPD9O Oqpx2BrABKb50Qe7lkmaVCG3OX551ySBIL LliWGgWDaU73N+4+CYqaWGT0tN7YD6 mFoNIAMufDtQbTfgkt9xEvmulycb7s5bqmZx- UuIQcW72EV+rsqJGqVmL3oJ0ikog79kU/ G8Ffj7oMLByNXrQWHi6SBhSTvgIpY EpSJ4tOhQGMA+bPv6+nr6vAAQwA54QrHdX LVS4VfWLny457u85JTxqmLvUizzodQjo0i/ HJ3pI8dXxS8o8exNk3RMQpt2MhpnAmAIDJ YCiWQ8+bTcgipzt2hYyOtNDwLYCUSJDMQBp 6lJGaZVThp74oQkehUc023FkpDqZN4SdofO24 cH2mRT3iC7OK8aq055+DkT1jnWFkrIR16G -----End PGP MESSAGE-----

Less than a month after Micah launched the Freedom of the Press Foundation's website, he received an encrypted email from an anonymous source. This triggered a sequence of events Micah would later recount at the *Intercept*.

Decrypted, the email read:

From: anon108@XXXXX
To: Micah Lee
Date: Fri, 11 Jan 2013

Micah,

I'm a friend. I need to get information securely to Laura Poitras and her alone, but I can't find an email/gpg key for her.

Can you help?

Micah didn't know it at the time, but a month earlier the same mysterious source had contacted another Freedom of the Press Foundation board member: Glenn Greenwald. The source wanted to have a private conversation with him and urged him to set up encryption. But the journalist kept brushing him off.

The source, who had introduced himself to Greenwald as "Cincinnatus," didn't give up easily. He went so far as to create a twelve-minute instructional video called "GPG for Journalists," which he uploaded to Vimeo in early January.

That tutorial — while painstakingly thorough — was utterly unwatchable. The narrator's voice, though discernibly male, was otherwise disguised with a low-tech pitch shifter. His words careened from note to note, as if he'd swallowed a Casio keyboard. On the screen, a diagram was drawn freehand using the primitive graphics editor MS Paint. It showed two wobbly green stick figures. The one on the left, labeled "SOURCE," stood next to a box that said: "message that could get source killed." The one on the right, labeled "JOURNO," wore a pink top hat. Between them was a menacing red scribble. It had a one-word caption: "INTERNET."

The narrator explained his mission: helping journalists shepherd private messages safely through the "untrusted environment" represented by the red scribble. As the video droned on, he seemed keenly aware that he'd have to fight to hold Greenwald's attention. Talking about password security, he quipped: "Pick a memorable quote that you don't have to write down that's meaningful to you but no one else knows. Like, 'Margaret Thatcher is 110 percent sexy.'" Near the end, he appealed to Greenwald's loathing for the federal agents who detained globetrotting documentarians like Laura. Using encryption, the video suggested playfully, was also "a really great way to piss off national security states and make your air travel more interesting."

It's unlikely Greenwald watched that far. Either way, the video didn't succeed at turning him on to crypto. In his book, Greenwald wrote about how the person he knew only as "Cincinnatus" described his mounting frustration.

"Here I am, ready to risk my liberty, perhaps even my life, to hand this guy thousands of Top Secret documents from the nation's most secretive agency — a leak that will produce dozens if not hundreds of huge journalistic scoops," the whistleblower reflected. "And he can't even be bothered to install an encryption program."

Undeterred, the mysterious source decided he had to approach someone else. He chose Laura. He'd seen *The Program* and knew she was working on a larger film about surveillance. He'd also read what Greenwald had written in *Salon* about her repeated detentions. He would later tell Laura,

> The surveillance you've experienced means you've been selected . . . every border you cross, every purchase you make, every call you dial, every cell phone tower you pass, friend you keep, article you write, site you visit, subject line you type, and packet you route, and even advertisement you see is in the hands of a system whose reach is unlimited, but whose safeguards are not. Your victimization by the NSA system means that you are well aware of the threat that unrestricted secret police pose for democracies. This is a story few but you can tell.

To get to Laura, the source decided to go through Micah. He assigned them both code names: DARKDIAMOND for Laura and SILVERSHOT for Micah. (He also had a name for Greenwald: COPPERCOMET.)

"He was pretty sure that Laura used PGP, but he didn't know a way to get her key and validate it," Micah recalled. "He figured that since I knew her, I probably had it." After all, it was clear from the Freedom of the Press website — where Micah had posted his fingerprint — that he and Laura were colleagues. On top of that, Micah seemed trustworthy. His public key had been vouched for by some of the most respected figures in the world of digital privacy. That made it a reliable node in the crowdsourced, decentralized verification system that encryption users call a "web of trust."

It's easy to go down a rabbit hole when you're talking about how to build trust in the digital world. That's why so much writing about blockchain is inscrutable. But the basic principle behind using a web of trust to leverage credibility is simple. In an online article explaining why it's so important, Henk Penning, a developer at Utrecht University, arrived at a conclusion that would please fans of *The Matrix*. He wrote:

> What can I trust, ultimately?
> The short answer is **nothing**. For the ultra-skeptics, there is no hope.

> ❏ you can't trust the things you did yesterday, because you can't trust your memory
> ❏ you can't trust software you didn't write or hardware you didn't build

❏ you can't overlook the possibility that [this website] is a fake, set up especially to lure you into using bad software

In other words: crypto nerds don't take trust for granted. The downside of that worldview? There's no such thing as too much paranoia. The community adheres to a modern version of the maxim Benjamin Franklin coined three centuries ago: "Three can keep a secret, if two of them are dead."

Hackers know that perfect secrecy — and by extension, perfect privacy — is impossible. The next-best thing is settling for strategies to reduce risks. That's what the mysterious source did when he contacted Greenwald, and once again when he decided to try Micah instead.

When Micah got the source's request, he sent Laura an encrypted version of the following message:

From: Micah Lee
To: Laura Poitras
Date: Sat, 12 Jan 2013

Hey Laura,

This person just sent me this GPG encrypted email. Do you want to respond? If you want to, and you need any help with using crypto, I'm happy to help.

Laura wrote back:

From: Laura Poitras
To: Micah Lee

Date: Sat, 12 Jan 2013

Hey Micah,

Thanks for asking. Sure, you can tell this person I can be reached with GPG at: XXXXX@gmail.com

I'll reply with my public key.

I'm also on jabber/OTR at:
XXXXX@jabber.org

I hope all is good with you!

Laura

The sender, of course, turned out to be Snowden. He was on the verge of communicating with Laura for the first time.

Even though Snowden appeared to be an experienced crypto user, Micah noted, his approach wasn't flawless. When the would-be whistleblower first contacted Micah, he'd forgotten to include his own public key. That meant Micah couldn't reply with an encrypted message. He had to send Snowden a regular plaintext email instead, and hope that no one was paying attention. (This appeared to be a momentary lapse on Snowden's part; in the how-to video he made for Greenwald, he noted that a source should always include "a copy of his public key, so the journalist can respond.")

"Everything wasn't perfect," Micah reflected. "But there

was no red flag, and I've gotten lots of emails from random anonymous people. I did pretty well, considering that I had no idea what the hell was going on."

This was an understatement. Micah was in the dark, utterly uninformed about the content of the communications he was brokering. That was fine with him, though. He knew Laura and believed in her work. That trust was enough. He didn't feel compelled to pry into the details.

"Whatever they were doing was sensitive, and I had no need to know," he later explained via the *Intercept*. "Whether you're working in the analog or digital world, this is one of the simplest and most important security practices: share secrets only with people who have to know. The fewer people who know a secret, the lower the chances are that it will be compromised."

Amid all that uncertainty, Snowden offered Micah one assurance. Someday, he said, Micah would be proud of the role he'd played in this clandestine endeavor.

Once Snowden reached Laura using encrypted email, the two of them took extra steps to harden the security of their conversations. Some unaddressed hazards remained. How could they be certain, for instance, that Laura wasn't under NSA surveillance? Her history of airport detentions meant federal officials had already taken an unwelcome interest in her work. What if her email had been compromised?

"Please confirm that no one has ever had a copy of your private key and that it uses a strong passphrase. Assume your adversary is capable of 1 trillion guesses per second," Snowden wrote to her.

Laura bought a laptop with cash. Using Tails to

anonymize her identity, she went online and created fresh communication tools: a new email address and keys for encrypted messages. She planned to use these only to correspond with Snowden, whom she knew at the time only as "Citizenfour." Apart from safeguarding their actual conversations, this gave Laura an added layer of protection. To prying eyes, she would appear anonymous, since these credentials had never been connected to her true name.

Still, there were other dangers. How could Citizenfour be sure he was exchanging information with Laura — rather than a hacker impersonating her? What if both Citizenfour and Laura had been tricked into speaking with a nefarious third party — an NSA agent, perhaps — who read their email before forwarding it to the intended destination, via what's known as a man-in-the-middle attack?

To avoid those dark possibilities, Citizenfour had to verify he'd received the right public key from Laura. He asked her to send Micah her new anonymous fingerprint — the forty-digit verification code — with instructions to post it on Twitter.

Laura sent Micah this encrypted email from her new account:

From: XXX@riseup.net
To: Micah Lee
Date: Mon, 28 Jan 2013

Hey Micah,

This is Laura Poitras.

Someone is trying to verify my fingerprint to this email. The person has proposed you tweet the fingerprint. Would you be able to tweet this to your acct:

1EBF 5F15 850C 540B 3142 F158 4BDD 496D 4C6C 5F25

Let me know if possible.

Thanks,
Laura

And so Micah tweeted the following:

Posting sensitive information on Twitter — that most public of forums — may sound counterintuitive as part of a security strategy. But it was smart.

Micah's tweet reassured Snowden that the fingerprint was coming from a trusted source. After all, Micah probably would have noticed, or heard from his followers, if someone had hacked his Twitter account.

Micah was the perfect person to act as a go-between. As a self-described "paranoid hacker kid," he'd spent years training for something like the Snowden moment. One of his favorite spare-time activities had been going to hacker conventions like Def Con and playing a digital version of capture the flag, with players competing to break into dummy accounts and steal the messages inside.

In retrospect, Micah realized those "games" had become his training for 2013, when things got very serious, very fast.

"I did this for years before I ever needed it," he explained. "It's a lot more important now that I work with real secrets, instead of just being a nerd. I think that using the tools before you need the tools is super important, because nobody ever knows when they are going to be dropped into a situation like this."

For Micah, who was keenly aware of how hackers operate, taking strong measures to protect himself had long been second nature. One of his most important tools was a USB stick loaded with Tails. Micah was careful about where he kept that flash drive, so no one could tamper with it. That meant he could plug it into his laptop and use it to boot up, secure in the knowledge that — even if someone had messed with his actual computer — the drive running his operating system hadn't been infected with malware.

Beyond that, Micah had another asset: he was incredibly trustworthy. As months passed, he would learn more about the Snowden situation. He kept quiet with his EFF colleagues, though surely they would have sympathized with the cause. Newly married, he told only his wife. He'd learned from a lawyer that spousal privilege would protect her from testifying against him.

Besides, he added, "It wouldn't be fair if crazy shit went down and she didn't even know."

Micah hoped that knowing what might come would help prepare her for sudden danger. Meanwhile, Snowden had taken the opposite strategy in his personal life. He'd kept his partner, Lindsay Mills, a twenty-eight-year-old performance artist and photographer, in the dark during during the saga of the box. This must have been a very lonely road for him — keeping dangerous secrets from the human he trusted most — but he did it to protect her from the authorities who would inevitably descend on their doorstep in Hawaii once he was gone.

If Mills knew nothing, there was nothing she could tell them. Of course, it's hard to fathom the kind of heartache that meant for them both. The media would go on to dissect Mills's life — her blog, her photos — with a scrutiny she never could have anticipated and certainly didn't deserve.

On June 7, after the first *Guardian* revelations hit, Mills posted, "Sick, exhausted, and carrying the weight of the world."

Micah felt some of that weight too as the news went live. His anxiety spiked. "This all was pretty stressful," he told us. "But it was most stressful for Laura and Glenn and Ed."

Like us and Laura, Micah worried about the possibility of a raid. What if the authorities showed up at his home? He began keeping the USB stick on his person at all times, even when he went out for a jog.

Micah described all this to us at a diner in Berkeley some three years later. It felt good to finally meet him in person, to swap stories from those tense and paranoid times. Back when it was all happening, there'd been no way out of our individual silos — we had to be strangers.

Laura was "totally smart," he said, to keep the players

separate. "Let's say that my house had gotten raided. I wouldn't be able to tell them about you guys. I didn't know you guys. It makes a lot of sense."

Did he think the NSA was watching him? Or even us?

"Obviously," he said. "They're watching everybody."

4.

American Amnesia

Power concedes nothing without a demand. It never did and it never will. — Frederick Douglass

On Independence Day, less than a month after the NSA leaks began, protesters gathered in more than eighty cities for "Restore the Fourth" rallies. The name was a double-reference to the July 4 holiday and the Fourth Amendment, which protects the rights of Americans to "be secure in their persons, houses, papers, and effects, against unreasonable searches and seizures."

In New York, a crowd descended on Union Square with colorful placards that read:

> *Stop Watching Me Masturbate*
> *The NSA Has TMI*
> *1984 Is Not an Instruction Manual*
> *Dance Like the NSA Is Watching*
> *Land of the Free: Nazi Germany*
> *Don't Track on Me*

NSA Doesn't Need to Know the Weird S@?T I'm Into

and

Hey, NSA, Can You Read This?
(with a cutout for the bearer's middle finger)

The performance artist and activist Reverend Billy, with his signature white suit, priest's collar, and bottle-blond pompadour, stood in front of a banner that said "Yes We Scan" and delivered an anti-surveillance sermon.

"We're here now, together, subscribing to a kind of courage! Now that we understand that the environment that we live in vacuums up our conversations, that invisible people are watching us all the time," he preached. "Now we know it! And we know that we must combat it with a new kind of activism!" Hundreds cheered as a gospel choir began singing from the Bill of Rights.

The privacy movement was gaining momentum. One sunny Saturday in late October, a crowd of thousands converged on Washington, DC, for another rally, timed to coincide with the twelfth anniversary of the Patriot Act. Organizers said it was the largest protest against mass surveillance in American history. Political observers were impressed by the scope. "It was as if the Tea Party and Occupy Wall Street had clasped hands," one MSNBC reporter reflected. More than one hundred groups joined forces to sponsor the march, from the ACLU to the conservative nonprofit FreedomWorks, along with the Libertarian and Green parties. Together, they formed a grassroots coalition called Stop Watching Us that — despite its name

— drew tons of attention, with media coverage from around the globe.

Demonstrators marched from Union Station to the Capitol Mall, brandishing signs that read "Unplug Big Brother" and "Read the US Constitution, Not My Email." Drummers kept time as they chanted: "Hey, hey! Ho, ho! Mass surveillance has got to go!" and "They say wiretap? We say fight back!" Others walked in silence, their mouths covered by strips of duct tape that read "NSA."

Gathered in front of a stage, they heard from Jesselyn Radack, a former Justice Department ethics adviser and a director at the Government Accountability Project, a non-profit that protects whistleblowers. Radack had visited Snowden in Russia two weeks earlier. She delivered a statement on his behalf.

"We are witnessing an American moment in which ordinary people from high school to high office stand up to oppose a dangerous trend in government," she read. "We declare that mass surveillance has no place in this country."

Snowden's speech ended with a warning to public officials: "*We* are watching *you!*"

For years, activists had predicted it would take a major cataclysm or scandal — what they called a "Privacy Chernobyl" — to galvanize the regular people against surveillance. Many saw the Snowden leaks as such a moment. They hoped that, years later, the protests of 2013 would be remembered as the start of a public outcry loud enough to force lasting change. There was an innocence in that idealism, a sense something new was possible.

But history pointed at a different outcome. The US government's track record of spying on its own citizens went back much further than the Snowden affair. The past is quickly forgotten; most living Americans, some 65 percent of the US population, were born after 1975. They weren't alive when public controversy exploded over the notorious federal surveillance program known as Cointelpro.

On March 8, 1971, while the nation was preoccupied by the "Fight of the Century" between Joe Frazier and Muhammed Ali, eight activists broke into an FBI field office on the outskirts of Philadelphia. They carted off all the files, then sent photocopies to the *Washington Post*, along with the Washington bureaus of the *Los Angeles Times* and *New York Times*. Keeping their true identities a secret, they called themselves the Citizens' Commission to Investigate the FBI.

But two of the newspapers balked. The *Los Angeles Times* and the *New York Times* sent the files right back to the government. This episode was later recounted in *The Burglary*, a book by *Washington Post* journalist Betty Medsger, who wrote groundbreaking stories based on the trove.

A torrent of headlines and televised news reports followed. They exposed the agency's counterintelligence program, or Cointelpro, a series of top-secret — and often illegal — operations aimed at monitoring and neutralizing activists. Authorized by FBI director J. Edgar Hoover, Cointelpro began in 1956 with a focus on disrupting supposed communists. Its mandate soon widened to include civil rights, black power, antiwar, feminist, and other advocacy groups, from the National Organization for Women and the NAACP to the Anti-Defamation League and the National Lawyers Guild.

One of Hoover's most infamous operations targeted the Rev. Dr. Martin Luther King Jr. After King gave his "I Have a Dream" speech on the Capitol Mall in 1963, Hoover's deputy — William Sullivan, the head of the FBI domestic intelligence division — wrote a memo about the young civil rights leader that echoed his boss's views. It said:

> We must mark [King] now, if we have not done so before, as the most dangerous Negro of the future in this Nation from the standpoint of communism, the Negro and national security.

Hoover ordered full surveillance of King, which included bugging his hotel rooms and recording his sexual encounters.

The next year, Congress passed the Civil Rights Act and King won the Nobel Peace Prize. Hoover was apoplectic. In a personal letter to Sullivan, he said he hoped King got his "just deserts." Soon after, Sullivan sent King an anonymous package. It contained a cassette tape — presumably recordings of King having sex — and a message that came to be known as the "suicide letter." It read in part:

> The American public . . . will know you for what you are — an evil, abnormal beast . . . There is only one way out for you. You better take it before your filthy, abnormal fraudulent self is bared to the nation.

That letter, a copy of which is preserved in the National Archives, was one of the most sinister artifacts of an FBI gone haywire. But it only represented a fraction of Cointelpro's transgressions. Another notorious episode was the assassination of Black Panther leader Fred Hampton,

slain by Chicago police officers in a raid coordinated with
— and later covered up by — the FBI. A paid Cointelpro
mole later confessed to slipping Hampton a sedative before
the raid.

During the fifteen years of Cointelpro, agents spied on
more than one million Americans, including Malcolm X,
John Lennon, James Baldwin, Jane Fonda, Yoko Ono, Abbie
Hoffman, and Muhammad Ali. Operatives broke into
hundreds of homes. They sent unsigned, slanderous letters
to activists' employers, trying to get them fired. They infiltrated grassroots organizations, spreading disinformation to
corrode trust between members, causing groups to splinter
apart, actively promoting violence that sometimes led to
murders.

One especially poisonous technique was called "bad-jack-
eting" or "snitch jacketing." Agents would single out an
activist, then circulate rumors or plant evidence suggesting
that person was an informant. The goal was for the "snitch"
to be shunned — or worse — by former allies who felt their
trust had been betrayed.

Though staggering in scope, the Cointelpro revelations were
part of a much larger picture. The first half of the 1970s saw a
huge wave of domestic surveillance disclosures. Americans
learned the army had been monitoring civilians and, soon after,
were rocked by the most infamous scandal of all: Watergate. In
August 1974, President Richard Nixon was forced to resign
amid public outrage over his illegal spying on the Democratic
Party. Meanwhile, the news about illegal surveillance kept
coming. Six months later, the *New York Times* revealed in a
front-page investigative scoop from reporter Seymour Hersh
that the CIA had violated its charter by running a domestic

intelligence operation against antiwar protesters and other activists, keeping files on at least 10,000 US citizens.

The national mood tipped, briefly, from horror to outrage. Agencies meant to protect Americans were persecuting them instead; clearly, the system was broken.

The following year marked the first-ever congressional investigation of federal intelligence agencies. Headed by Senator Frank Church (D-ID), an eleven-member, bipartisan committee held 126 hearings, called 800 witnesses, and studied more than 100,000 documents. Its deliberations laid much of the groundwork for the modern-day debate over domestic spying. Committee members were distressed to see how civil liberties had been trampled in the name of national security. With almost uncanny foresight, they called for policies to rein in the intelligence agencies. During one particularly prescient hearing, Senator Walter Mondale (D-MN) addressed the NSA director, Lieutenant General Lew Allen Jr., telling him:

> What we have to deal with is whether this incredibly powerful and impressive institution that you head could be used by President 'A' in the future to spy upon the American people, to chill and interrupt political dissent. And it is my impression that the present condition of the law makes that entirely possible. And therefore we need to, in my opinion, very carefully define the law, spell it out so that it is clear what your authority is and it is also clear what your authority is not.

The Church Committee investigations would go on to reveal, among other abuses, a pair of secret, overreaching

NSA surveillance programs. The first, code-named "Shamrock," strayed from its initial mission — intercepting international telegrams related to foreign targets — to collect the telegrams of selected Americans. The second, called "Minaret," expanded the NSA's watch list to include Vietnam War protesters.

In the spring of 1976, the committee released a two-foot-thick final report. Some of its most scathing commentary was reserved for Cointelpro, including a passage that read:

> Many of the techniques used would be intolerable in a democratic society even if all of the targets had been involved in violent activity, but Cointelpro went far beyond that . . . the Bureau conducted a sophisticated vigilante operation aimed squarely at preventing the exercise of First Amendment rights of speech and association.

The committee concluded that domestic spying had thrived, growing monstrous, because there was little oversight to constrain it. In other words: no one was watching the watchers.

"Intelligence agencies have undermined the constitutional rights of citizens, primarily because checks and balances designed by the framers of the Constitution to assure accountability have not been applied," the report stated.

In the years that followed, legislators tried to regulate the agencies with a system of safeguards. They created a permanent oversight body, the Senate Select Committee on Intelligence. They passed the Foreign Intelligence Surveillance Act (FISA), requiring agents who wanted to spy on Americans or foreign nationals to get permission from a new judicial body, the FISA Court. Presidents Gerald R. Ford and Jimmy Carter issued executive orders — in 1976 and 1978, respectively — aimed at tightening regulation of the intelligence agencies.

Not everyone was thrilled by the changes. "Periods of sin and excess are commonly followed by spasms of remorse and moralistic overreaction," harrumphed famed conservative Robert Bork, who'd served as Nixon's solicitor general, in a *Wall Street Journal* op-ed. "The repentance of the hungover reveler is standard comic fare."

But Bork needn't have worried; the age of regret didn't last long. Soon the sense of urgency sparked by the Church Committee faded. Meanwhile, the FISA Court, operating in the shadows with closed-door sessions and classified opinions, got a reputation for rubber-stamping surveillance applications. In the first thirty-three years of its life, the secret court would authorize 33,942 warrants and turn down just twelve, or .03 percent, of all requests.

Then came the day that changed everything. On September 11, 2001, a pair of hijacked aircraft brought down the World Trade Center. Weeks later, as fires still burned in the wreckage at Ground Zero, Congress passed the USA Patriot Act: a massive expansion of surveillance powers in the name of national security.

Later, the Brookings Institution fellow Stuart Taylor Jr. would put it succinctly:

> The emergence of this new menace to America and its allies brought an upsurge in political and public support for aggressive surveillance of potential terrorists, and a muting of the concerns that had arisen in the 1970s

about the past sins and excessive zeal of US intelligence agencies.

Fast-forward to 2013. The Patriot Act helped pave the way for the NSA to collect Americans' phone records and emails. Snowden believed it was time, once again, to rein in the intelligence agencies — not just because of how the government was violating citizens' privacy in that particular moment, but also for the sake of the future.

Inevitably, another catastrophe would reawaken calls for more surveillance, just as September 11 had. Would all the old lessons be forgotten?

In his June 9 video on the *Guardian's* website, Snowden put it like this:

> And [in] the months ahead, the years ahead . . . a new leader will be elected. They'll flip the switch, say that because of the crisis, because of the dangers that we face in the world, you know, some new and unpredicted threat, we need more authority. We need more power. And there will be nothing the people can do at that point to oppose it, and it will be turnkey tyranny.

Snowden's warning described a perilous future, but savvy listeners also heard something else: the past. The phrase "turnkey tyranny," in particular, invoked the words of Senator Church, who said forty-three years earlier on *Meet the Press*:

> If a dictator ever took charge in this country, the technological capacity that the intelligence community has

given the government could enable it to impose total tyranny, and there would be no way to fight back because the most careful effort to combine together in resistance to the government, no matter how privately it was done, is within the reach of the government to know.

For scholars and privacy activists, 2013 felt like a rerun of the mid-1970s. Snowden wasn't the only one who saw those parallels. The Electronic Frontier Foundation called for a new Church Committee, a campaign that was later joined by a dozen of the original committee's members.

Nothing quite that drastic happened. There were flickers of progress, though. In 2015, Congress passed the USA Freedom Act, which aimed to make the FISA court more transparent and forbade the collection of bulk internet and phone records.

Yet the law was imperfect. Telecom companies were still collecting metadata, which was discovered in 2018. The NSA had to purge hundreds of millions of calls and texts. "Telecom companies hold vast amounts of private data on Americans," US senator Ron Wyden (D-OR.) said. "This incident shows these companies acted with unacceptable carelessness, and failed to comply with the law when they shared customers' sensitive data with the government."

The Snowden revelations also seemed to drive a temporary wedge between Silicon Valley and Washington. Tech companies rushed to assert their trustworthiness, integrating more privacy-friendly protocols and reassuring consumers they wouldn't sell them out to the feds.

At the same time, skeptics worried that some of the

privacy-friendly poses struck by tech firms distracted from deeper issues. "By forming temporary alliances with Google, Facebook and [others], privacy activists gave them a PR platform to show the world that they are also concerned about their users' privacy — rather than to actively challenging their business practices and informing the public about the essential role they have played — voluntarily or not — in the NSA's regime," wrote German media scholar Till Wäscher.

In 2016, the popular messaging service WhatsApp began using end-to-end encryption to protect users' communications. The same year, tensions rose as Apple defied a federal court order to help the FBI break into an iPhone belonging to one of the perpetrators of a San Bernardino mass shooting that killed fourteen people.

"The same engineers who built strong encryption into the iPhone to protect our users would, ironically, be ordered to weaken those protections and make our users less safe," said Apple CEO Tim Cook, who later made "privacy is a human right" his public mantra. Justice Department officials derided the company's refusal to cooperate, calling it a "marketing strategy."

On the fifth anniversary of the leaks, Snowden told the *Guardian* he had no regrets. Public awareness, he said, was the most important outcome of his actions. He explained:

> The government and corporate sector preyed on our ignorance. But now we know. People are aware now. People are still powerless to stop it but we are trying. The revelations made the fight more even.

But how aware were Americans, really? Less than two years after the NSA revelations, the talk show host John Oliver dispatched a camera crew to Times Square. Interviewing passersby, they found most could not accurately identify Edward Snowden. Folks remembered some kind of leak had happened, but not what it was or why it mattered. (They did, however, express grave anxiety over the possibility that government officials might be looking at, as the correspondent put it, their "dick pics.")

Around the same time, nearly half of Americans reported they were "not very concerned" or "not at all concerned" about government surveillance, according to a Pew Research Center survey.

Given our history, none of this was surprising. After the initial outrage of the mid-1970s, when a groundswell of public concern spurred a wave of reform, everyone went back to business as usual. That cycle is repeating again. What briefly looked like the start of a movement in America was quickly overtaken by numbness and resignation. Observers called the phenomenon "surveillance fatigue" or the rise of "so-what surveillance."

Gore Vidal once described America as "the United States of Amnesia," but forgetfulness knows no borders. Short-term thinking is human nature. It's why we've spent more than four decades ignoring climate change — allowing a catastrophe to become inevitable, even when we had time to avert it.

Meanwhile, spying has become normalized, even domesticated. Ordinary people have grown more accustomed than ever to surrendering private information, often for the sake of convenience. Even when the 2016 election ended in a civil libertarians' nightmare — the presidency of Donald J. Trump — it did little to awaken public concerns that the surveillance juggernaut built by past administrations would finally stir to life.

5.

The Panopticon in the Parlor

There's gonna be a meter on your bed
That will disclose
What everybody knows.
— Leonard Cohen, "Everybody Knows"

On a September night in 2017, *New York Times* tech columnist Farhad Manjoo and his wife were getting ready to sleep when a blood-curdling shriek arose from the bedside.

It was Alexa.

"The voice assistant began to wail, like a child screaming in a horror-movie dream," Manjoo later recalled. His Twitter followers greeted the news with sarcasm and satirical advice:

"You have an always-on, deep-learning supercomputer node in your house always listening and you are surprised it screams?" wrote one.

"Why voluntarily have CIA spy tech in your home?" asked another.

"If I were you, I'd keep all the network access wires in one place and keep an axe nearby," advised a third.

Suspicions about Alexa were already running high; a hacker had recently demonstrated how an Echo could be transformed into a wiretap. Over the following months, Alexa's odd behavior continued. Users reported that she was emitting fits of unprompted laughter. Some called it "creepy" or "witch-like." Others heard her cackling away in the dark, after they'd gone to bed. Then things got very weird at a home in Portland, Oregon, that had Amazon smart speakers in every room.

"My husband and I would joke and say 'I bet these devices are listening to what we're saying," recalled the woman who lived there. In May 2018, she learned the speakers had done more than listen. They'd actually recorded ambient household chatter — including a conversation about hardwood floors — and emailed audio files of it to one of her husband's employees. That was especially jarring because Amazon had claimed the Echo, while always listening, only starts recording when triggered by a spoken "wake" command — usually the word "Alexa."

Amazon dismissed the malfunctions as rare glitches. Meanwhile, a public debate ignited on social media. What did it mean that millions of citizens had installed always-on listening devices in their own homes? Did the popularity of the Amazon Echo mark a new frontier in the domestication of surveillance — a panopticon in every parlor? Beloved for obeying commands to play songs, check the weather, and carry out a litany of other benign tasks, smart speakers suddenly seemed to have darker, less benevolent potential. A *New Yorker* cartoon transformed the Echo Dot into a sinister hockey puck with a red halo, slanted eyebrows and a nefarious "hahahahahaha" hovering overhead. It had an Amazon smile logo for a mouth. Inside were rows of pointy shark teeth.

The Amazon Echo came to market in November 2014, just a year and a half after Snowden's revelations began stoking concerns about mass surveillance. Consumers couldn't get enough of it. By May 2017, Amazon had sold an estimated 10.7 million of the Alexa-powered devices. Overall sales of smart speakers that year — including Google Home, the lagging competitor to Amazon Echo — hit nearly 25 million. Market researchers estimated that in 2020 three-quarters of American homes would have smart speakers and that, by the following year, the number of voice-activated assistants could easily rival earth's human population.

As Amazon saturates the market with new smart speakers, it also works to expand the capabilities of those it has already sold via software updates. The "smarter" they get, the better such devices become at extracting continuous — and ever-greater — profits from users worldwide. The writer Shoshana Zuboff has referred to this model as "surveillance capitalism," and most ordinary folk have more to fear from it than they do from the NSA. A panopticon in every parlor, after all, is good for business.

Amazon's patents offer what could be a sneak preview of the future. They include technologies to mine ambient speech for keywords and share them with advertisers, even in the absence of a "wake" command. If a device overhears you saying, "I like the beach," for example, you could be targeted with ads for sunblock and towels.

Amazon's patent diagrams illustrate the process like this:

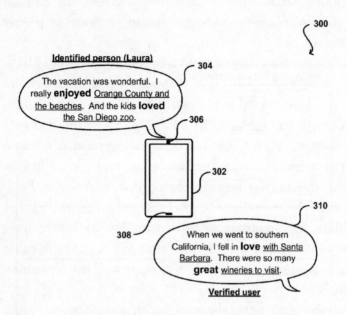

Identified person (Laura) — 304

The vacation was wonderful. I really **enjoyed** Orange County and the beaches. And the kids **loved** the San Diego zoo.

306

302

308

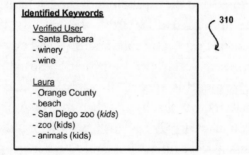

310

When we went to southern California, I fell in **love** with Santa Barbara. There were so many **great** wineries to visit.

Verified user

Identified Keywords
310

Verified User
- Santa Barbara
- winery
- wine

Laura
- Orange County
- beach
- San Diego zoo (*kids*)
- zoo (kids)
- animals (kids)

300

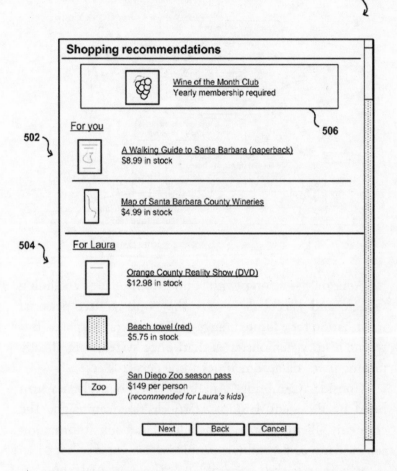

Amazon has also patented a technology that analyzes the human voice to determine, among other things, ethnic origin, gender, age, health, and mental state. "A cough or sniffle, or crying, may indicate that the user has a specific physical or emotional abnormality," the patent explains. It includes this illustration:

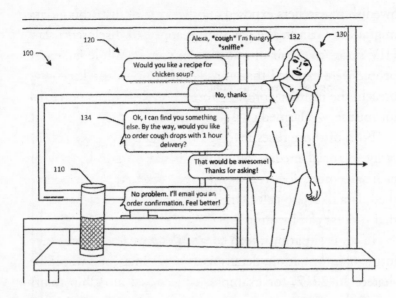

Amazon — along with other tech giants including Google and Facebook — say they only collect personal information for a limited range of commercial purposes. But recent history demonstrates that, once systems are already mining users' data, sometimes a line gets crossed.

Consider Cambridge Analytica, the political data firm hired by President Trump's 2016 election campaign. The company illicitly obtained detailed Facebook information on as many as 87 million people whose votes it hoped to sway with targeted political ads. The potential abuse of profile data had long been debated, as everyone from credit card companies to health insurers showed a keen interest in Facebook. But this time the victim wasn't just individuals. It was democracy.

Two weeks after the *New York Times* and the *Observer* of London unearthed the Cambridge Analytica scandal,

Swedish researchers exposed another case of disturbing data migration: Grindr, the gay dating app, had disclosed users' HIV status to a pair of outside companies. While far fewer people were exposed than those caught up in the Facebook breach, the intimacy of the information — and its potential for misuse — alarmed civil libertarians.

Both of those cases involved data that users gave voluntarily to social media companies, based on trust. But that tacit agreement doesn't always happen in an era where people shed data like skin cells. (In the case of DNA data-banking, that process can be quite literal.)

In some situations, tech companies have given away very intimate information, details users never imagined would be shared. In 2017, for example, police used an Ohio man's pacemaker data to charge him with burning down his own house to collect on the insurance — a literal case of the telltale heart.

Since smart speakers' microphones are always turned on, privacy advocates worry about them becoming wiretaps for law enforcement. That sounds alarmist until you look back at 2006, when federal agents got permission to use a cellphone as a "roving bug." What would prevent them from making a similar request involving an Amazon Echo or any other smart device with a microphone or sensors?

The spread of networked devices — the so-called internet of things — could someday give police easy access to the most private parts of our lives. Law enforcement already has a formidable array of surveillance technologies, ranging from license plate readers to the cell site simulators nicknamed "stingrays" that mimic mobile phone towers to facial recognition and access to credit card transactions — an area of data that is mushrooming as some areas of the country move towards a cashless economy. Meanwhile, Amazon has quietly been licensing its own facial recognition software, called Rekognition, to law enforcement agencies. In November 2018, alarmed members of Congress wrote a letter to Jeff Bezos, demanding to know more about how Rekognition was being used. Weeks later, a new Amazon patent application went public. It described a neighborhood surveillance system, made up of networked doorbell cameras that recognize "suspicious" people and call the police.

Alexa has already had a few brushes with the law. While investigating a 2015 murder in a hot tub, the police department of Bentonville, Arkansas, served Amazon with a search warrant for recordings from a nearby Echo. Reporters at *The Information* broke the news, calling it "what may be the first case of its kind." The suspect agreed to release the recordings and was later exonerated. Three years later, a New Hampshire judge made a similar demand, ordering Amazon to release recordings from an Echo sitting in the kitchen where two women were murdered.

Exercise tracker data — which can include users' heart rates, locations, and distances traveled — is showing up in courtrooms as evidence related to charges of sexual assault, personal injury, and homicide. In a Connecticut murder case, prosecutors obtained the victim's FitBit records to build a case against her husband, who claimed a masked intruder had shot her when the device showed she was still walking around.

The internet of things is a gold mine for police. Researchers are working to expand its applications for law enforcement. At Champlain University in Vermont, graduate students dedicated a semester to "Internet of Things Forensics," studying the

Nest thermostat and other devices to see how they could help criminal investigations. A program description praised the "diversity and usefulness" of networked objects — ranging from "routers that connect a laptop to the internet" to "a crockpot (from WEMO) and slippers (from 24eight)."

Back when Alexa's random laughter was creeping out unsuspecting Echo users, the *Today* show ran a segment on the device.

"Maybe it's just Jeff Bezos, the richest man on planet earth, having a good laugh at all of us behind the scenes," Carson Daly joked. Then he turned to his fellow hosts. "Do you guys have an Alexa? Where is it in your house?"

"In the kitchen!" replied Savannah Guthrie. "And all I really do is ask what time it is, 'cause I'm too lazy to, like, get up and look at the microwave."

Another host, Craig Melvin, interjected: "Are you not worried that she's listening on your conversations?"

"Well, our house is real boring," Guthrie replied. "What's she going to hear? Like, 'Don't touch that!'" she exclaimed, feigning desperation and lurching forward, as if to keep a small child from getting into some kind of trouble.

Everyone at the table laughed. By that point, most of America seemed to have similar feelings about surveillance. The argument went something like: "Why should I care if anyone's listening to me? I'm not breaking the law. I'm boring. I have nothing to hide."

But that's not true. Everyone has something to hide — even if it's not illegal behavior. Everyone has done things they wouldn't wish broadcast to the public. Consider the Martin Luther King sex tapes and ask yourself: would you want other people to hear you in flagrante delicto? Or using the bathroom?

Beyond that, consider all the mundane "secrets" our culture expects you to keep, from your Social Security number to your email password and debit card PIN. In the wrong hands — or just the wrong situation — any of that data could be used to make your life miserable. What if your personal information could be used to determine your credit score or ability to get a loan or insurance?

History shows us how the most basic information — such as where you live and where your ancestors came from — can be used to serve the paranoid and destructive whims of political leaders in moments of crisis.

During World War II, the US government secretly used census data to target Japanese Americans, who were shipped to internment camps in one of the most shameful civil rights abuses in the nation's history. The Census Bureau was forbidden by law to share information about individuals, but there were loopholes. Census officials lied for decades afterwards, claiming the bureau hadn't been involved, afraid the public would lose faith and stop participating in census-related activities.

Echoes of that tension were felt in March 2018, when federal officials announced the 2020 US Census would ask participants to disclose their citizenship status. Immigrants were alarmed. Many were already shaken by Trump's plan, announced six months earlier, to phase out Deferred Action for Childhood Arrivals, or DACA, which shielded people who had arrived in the United States as children from deportation. For DACA recipients, registering for the program had felt like a great risk. They trusted that the federal government would keep its word and not use the information they provided to deport them.

There's another reason ordinary people — folks with "nothing to hide" — should care about privacy. Surveillance has a chilling effect on speech and other forms of human expression. It is a culture-killer.

The novelist J. M. Coetzee, who grew up under apartheid in South Africa, once wrote, "Censorship looks forward to the day when writers will censor themselves and the censor himself can retire." The same principle applies to many systems of civic monitoring. In the perfect surveillance state, officers are no longer needed — a society polices itself. These means of control grow even more powerful when the government won't disclose the criteria for surveillance, as it does with "no-fly" lists restricting air travel. If people are scared of being spied on or punished — but don't know exactly what criteria will trigger that — they become especially malleable, willing to avoid a wide range of behaviors to reduce the risk.

Four months after the first Snowden leaks, the literary organization PEN surveyed American writers on how the revelations impacted their lives. The results were unsettling. Writers worried they were being monitored. Many admitted to censoring themselves or feeling reluctant to write, speak, or do research about politically sensitive subjects online. Topics that might make them targets, they speculated, included mass incarceration, the drug wars, sexual assault in the military, anti-American sentiment overseas, the Occupy movement, and the NSA leaks themselves.

"I have felt that even to comment on the Snowden case in an email would flag my email as worthy of being looked at," one anonymous respondent wrote.

PEN's researchers were disturbed by these responses. But what upset them even more was what, they feared, writers *wouldn't* say. As their report explained:

> Part of what makes self-censorship so troubling is the impossibility of knowing precisely what is lost to society because of it. We will never know what books or articles may have been written that would have shaped the world's thinking on a particular topic if they are not written because potential authors are afraid that their work would invite retribution.

> This idea isn't new. The so-called "chilling effects doctrine" emerged through legal decisions in cases related to anti-communist state measures in the 1950s and 60s. It urged the courts to exercise "suspicion" over any practices that "might deter" citizens from exercising their First Amendment rights freely.

After the Snowden revelations, there was a sudden drop in online traffic to terrorism-related Wikipedia articles, according to research published by the *Berkeley Technology Law Journal*. The articles included entries titled "dirty bomb," "Al Qaeda," "improvised explosive device," "nuclear enrichment," "extremism," and "suicide attack." It's possible that terrorists decided to stop using Wikipedia — but more likely that the public was afraid.

Other researchers noticed "chilling effects" when studying Google search traffic for privacy-sensitive search terms around the same period. Yet another noted more internet users participating in "privacy-enhancing activities."

As the Harvard professor Neil Richards put it: "Shadowy regimes of surveillance corrode the constitutional commitment to intellectual freedom that lies at the heart of most theories of political freedom in a democracy." Well-informed citizens are the lifeblood of a healthy society. They need the ability to think, read, write, and communicate privately, without feeling like they're being watched all the time.

In his 1968 novel *Desert Solitaire*, Edward Abbey wrote:

> A man could be a lover and defender of the wilderness without ever in his lifetime leaving the boundaries of asphalt, powerlines, and right-angled surfaces. We need wilderness whether or not we ever set foot in it. We need a refuge even though we may never need to set foot in it. We need the possibility of escape as surely as we need hope; without it the life of the cities would drive all men into crime or drugs or psychoanalysis.

If Abbey were alive, he'd be distressed by how much of our lives are monitored. Technology's capacity to mine the most intimate details of our lives has been growing rapidly. At the same time, the quest to "see all and know all" — a goal the government once called "total information awareness" — is intruding on some of the wild places where the human spirit can be free.

Society evolves when people can test boundaries and experiment with ways of living outside the mainstream. In a climate of total surveillance, such innovations would halt. The culture would stagnate and conformity would reign.

Consider the partial legalization of marijuana. If America were a perfect surveillance state — a despot's dream — it would have been impossible. Intermediate steps and experiments would have been quashed at every turn.

In the days after Edward Snowden's first leaks, the security researcher Moxie Marlinspike referred to that process in a blog post called "We Should All Have Something to Hide."

"Imagine if there were an alternate dystopian reality where law enforcement was 100% effective, such that any potential law offenders *knew* they would be immediately identified, apprehended, and jailed," he wrote. "How could people have decided that marijuana should be legal, if nobody had ever used it?"

Laws and norms, after all, don't change overnight. Reform pushes upward like grass through concrete. Social progress often follows a similar pattern. It starts with a few pioneers who see a possible benefit in a forbidden action and try it out. Their behavior spreads to artists and members of the counterculture. Then it gets big among city-dwellers and starts cropping up on social media. Soon everyone knows someone doing it. As minds begin to shift, legislators take notice. One state changes its rules, then a few more. Maybe the issue goes to the Supreme Court and, with the justices' sanction, the law of the land transforms.

Consider the last half-century of progress in civil rights in America. Interracial marriage wasn't fully legalized in this country until 1967. Gay marriage became legal and recognized in all fifty US states in 2015. Both developments happened incrementally.

The law is imperfect. For that reason, civil disobedience

— and ordinary citizens' right to question power — determine a democracy's capacity to evolve. That's especially true in an era when technology has put sophisticated media tools in so many hands. It's another reason ordinary people should care about mass state surveillance, as Kirsten Johnson, the documentary filmmaker, explained in one of our interviews.

"We are all camerapeople now," Kirsten said explained. "Everybody."

Circumstances can suddenly transform anyone with a smartphone into a citizen journalist. If you film a political demonstration or action by the police, you may end up possessing information that powerful interests would like to suppress. Something similar, after all, happened to Laura Poitras. She began her adult life as a chef. After she started making films with strong political themes, she became a target for government harassment. In other words: this stuff can happen to anyone.

Smartphone-wielding citizens were arrested for filming the deaths of Philando Castile, Eric Garner, Freddie Gray, and Alton Sterling. In Ferguson, Missouri, civilians were also detained for filming officers after the fatal police shooting of Michael Brown.

"The possibility of citizen journalism is thrilling, but we're also seeing this pushback around if you are the person who provided the video information; there's pressure on you from power structures," Kirsten continued. "For me that's a very critical part of this next phase of history, the way in which we are addressing how to empower people to use their cameras to speak about abuses of power but also to do it in a way where they are personally protected."

~

"The concept of surveillance is ingrained in our beings," the artist and professor Hasan Elahi once said. "God was the original surveillance camera."

For millennia, humans have believed that a superior intelligence — one with the power to reward and punish — was watching over them. The devout follow religious law because God is the ultimate spy.

In the secular world, watching people means you can gather enough data to build patterns. Then you can anticipate — and perhaps shape — future behavior. That means surveillance is never only about watching. It's an expression of power.

Intensive monitoring is cropping up in all sorts of human relationships. Domestic abusers have started spying on their spouses with technology designed to monitor kids. In the workplace, a modern strain of Taylorism has taken root. To extract maximum efficiency from workers, employers watch their every move. Walmart, America's largest retailer, patented audio-collecting technology to spy on cashiers. Amazon patented a bracelet that could track warehouse workers and deliver a sensory buzz whenever they make mistakes. Startups in Stockholm, Sweden, have been embedding microchips under employees' skin. In River Falls, Wisconsin, a company called Three Square Market created a similar program, giving participants T-shirts that said "I Got Chipped." Its CEO, Patrick McMullan, said he was eager to provide similar chips — in the form of wristbands or implants — to prisons, hospitals, and restaurants. He envisioned a future of networked bodies called "the internet of people." Companies could use that system, he added, to enforce workplace protocol.

"If (employees) haven't washed their hands, they can't

unlock the door," McMullan explained. "If you went to a restaurant, wouldn't you have a little more peace of mind if they were doing that?"

The idea of a boss who microchips workers — and locks them in the bathroom if they don't follow the rules — shouldn't give anyone peace of mind.

In the realm of law enforcement, predictive software is already making the world look a little more like Philip K. Dick's "The Minority Report," the 1956 science fiction short story that became a Spielberg film. Pentagon-backed research for predicting war casualties has been adapted into technology that law enforcement agencies use to forecast crime. Sold by a firm called PredPol, the software has been compared by critics to the widely discredited "broken windows" theory of policing. They note that it perpetuates discrimination and does not predict white-collar crime.

Meanwhile, Palantir, the $20 billion data analytics firm cofounded by Peter Thiel, has drawn protests for selling its services to ICE and the NYPD. (Meanwhile, executives raised eyebrows by sponsoring "thirteen-course tasting-menu lunches with lobster tail and sashimi at headquarters" as the company hemorrhaged money, a show of what critics dubbed "Palantir Entitlement Syndrome.")

To understand the ramifications of domestic spying, look to China, the world's most fully realized surveillance state. In Xinjiang province, authorities have collected residents' blood types, DNA samples, fingerprints, and iris scans. In Hangzhou, citizens with bad credit have been barred from booking fares on planes and bullet trains. Meanwhile, Beijing officials are scaling up local blacklists. The goal, according to the government's website, is a future where untrustworthy people are "unable to move even a single step."

6.

The Tree

The odds are against us, but odds never matter when you win.
— Edward L. Snowden, in an encrypted email to
Laura Poitras, May 23, 2013

Dale

For years, Jess and I discussed that brittle summer of 2013. We hoped to someday share this story, plugging a gap in the historical record to help humanize the narrative behind Snowden's monumental leak. I was also aware that I had pulled Jess into a certifiably crazy situation without her knowledge. She'd agreed to receive Snowden's box because she trusted me. I wanted to help her make sense of it all.

Yet I confess: I wasn't enthusiastic about approaching Laura. She'd been adamant that the behind-the-scenes story could only be told at some distant point in the future, but then she did an interview with the journalist Peter Maass for the *New York Times Magazine*. His article alluded to how the material had traveled.

I connected with Laura using Tails and an encrypted messaging program. I wasn't supposed to take a picture of my computer's screen — I'd never done this before — but that night I felt compelled to document.

I'd used a camera to take those pictures, so afterwards I removed the memory card and hid it. Weeks passed without word from Laura. Sometimes I booted up Tails and tried to ping her using Pidgin, a chat program, bolstered with a plug-in for encrypted messaging. A purple pigeon icon would appear and stare back blankly, as if to emphasize the 3:00 a.m. silence. Before the Snowden story broke, Laura had always been around, whenever I checked in. Now that anchor was gone. I couldn't travel to Germany that year. Writing deadlines continued to haunt me. Work had been bedeviling Laura too. On December 12, she emailed, "Sorry I've been out of touch — I've been slammed . . . I keep waiting for things to calm down, but they never do."

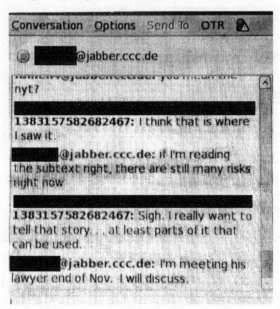

1383157582682467: Great. I want to visit you around then or after, probably early Dec. We can talk about in person.

▮▮▮▮▮jabber.ccc.de: ok, sounds good. it is really something that needs to be discussed in person.

1383157582682467: For certain. Over good German food! I had better ride my bike a lot before I visit.

In the summer of 2014, I finally made it to Berlin. One afternoon, in a back alley in the old Eastern Sector, Snowden stared down at me from street art wheat-pasted high on a wall.

That night Laura and I communicated using Tails. She told me to find her at Soho House Berlin, a members-only club. From what I knew of Laura, the choice sounded surprisingly upscale — but her rationale turned out to be unpretentious and practical. Joining Soho House was a long, complicated process, which made it hard for NSA agents, who are transferred often, to gain admission. For that reason, she held all of her meetings about sensitive topics there.

I didn't sleep well that night. The next afternoon, I caught a taxi, then kept looking over my shoulder to be sure I wasn't followed. I arrived early.

Soho House was an intriguing choice. The eight-story massive Bauhaus building was constructed in 1928 as a department store. After the Nazis took power, they seized it from its Jewish owners to use as a headquarters for Hitler Youth. The Allies bombed Berlin, but the building survived. Later, it housed an office for senior Stasi officials. After the Berlin Wall fell, the building was returned the original owners' heirs, then sold to Soho House.

I sat on a bench in the lobby. A tan-colored Great Dane lay just outside, tethered to a rail. Each time the front door opened, the dog's eyes met mine. I said "hello." The dog cocked his head, seeming to sense my anxiety. The appointed meeting time came and went. The dog left with its master.

Finally Laura showed up. "I think I had the only cabbie in Berlin who doesn't know where Soho House is located," she said. An elevator whisked us to an upper floor, where we ascended a stairwell. We emerged on the roof and were seated at a table near a long blue-green-lit reflecting pool. Euro techno-funk played from discreet speakers — easy to ignore if you desired conversation, loud enough to drown out your words if you didn't want to be overheard. We ordered drinks. I forget what Laura got, but I had a Żubrówka vodka martini.

Laura asked whether I'd followed her instructions to burn the shipping box in which Snowden's material had traveled to Brooklyn.

"No," I replied.

"Good. Where is it?" she asked.

I began telling her the location of the box and its contents. Before three words could escape my mouth, she raised a hand.

"I don't want to know," she said.

We ordered food. I had another Żubrówka. The rooftop offered a nearly 360-degree view of the city. To the west was the Fernsehturm, the lofty television tower near the Alexanderplatz. All of Berlin surrounded us in the long dusk.

Then we resumed a conversation I'd begun the year before, via Tails, when she was in Berlin and I was in New York. The topic: the box. Jess and I had been aching to tell the story of that tense summer. We hoped to fill in the historical record and help to humanize the narrative around a monumental leak.

Laura wasn't ready. "There are still many risks right now," she said.

I didn't understand how a human narrative about the box would create liabilities. Laura was working to finish her film *Citizenfour*. She said the big obstacle was "source protection." I wondered if there was some way to assuage that concern. We went around and around. I reminded her: Obama had left most of his promises about transparency unfulfilled. More leaks were likely to come.

"Others have to learn from what happened," I explained. Laura was unmoved. Our conversation vacillated between the Snowden saga and personal matters, the stuff of our lives — all at a searing level of emotion. As I rode back to my hotel in a taxi, I felt like throwing up.

Time passed. *Citizenfour* was released and won an Oscar. Jess and I had mostly gone back to living our normal lives.

Then, in March 2016, Laura sent an email inviting me and Jess to the New York branch of Soho House, where we dined with her, Trevor Timm, and another friend. Halfway through the meal Laura surprised us. She announced it was time for us to tell our story.

We asked: why now? Laura said some of the danger had dissipated. The most sensitive stories from the Snowden archive had already made it into the press and, meanwhile, other folks involved in the process were starting to talk. Greenwald had written a book; Gellman had one under contract. She didn't think it would be fair to ask us to keep our silence and, as a documentarian, she understood the urge to get it all down for posterity. We asked her if we could do some interviews with her about those tumultuous months, and she agreed. She also asked to review any sections of our work that might raise security or source-protection issues. That wasn't a problem.

From Laura's perspective, I realize I've probably said too much about our personal involvement, but there was no other way to tell this story. It explains her motivation.

"You were the person I trusted to be able to do what I needed to do," she said later. "There was nobody else I could ask." She also reminded me that she had asked me more than once to travel to Hong Kong with her to help break the Snowden story. "I invited you," she said. "So you have to include that. Don't censor it."

I won't.

Friends have asked: do I regret declining Laura's original invitation to travel to Hong Kong with her and meet Snowden? The answer is always no. At the time, I was dealing with profound depression over a book I had written about my father. But to a greater degree, I knew that, as a cultural journalist, this just wasn't my story — much like Laura, a filmmaker, knew the leaks couldn't come out as a film and that she needed help from news reporters. The project belonged to her and Greenwald, along with the other people whom she and Snowden entrusted to tell it. I chose not to immerse in what turned out to be a history-making drama — but I'm happy with the role I played.

Besides, it wasn't just journalism. It was life.

Jessica

Ever since I received the box, whenever a new book or movie promised an unabridged history of the leaks, I have wondered anxiously, *Will the box be in there?* And then I thought, *Better go cover the picnic table again.*

Despite my worries, I hoped this missing fragment of the story would surface someday. To me it reveals the humanness — the flaws and messiness bound up with idealism and courage — of Snowden's whole endeavor. It also testifies to the power of trust. It shows how friendship and good faith can prevail over great adversity. Snowden trusted Laura, who trusted Dale, who trusted me. That thread was strong enough to bind strangers together. It enabled something remarkable to happen.

I'll always wonder why Snowden used the pseudonym B. Manning with his return address on the box. I puzzled over it with a few people close to the situation. Why would such a smart guy have risked exposing himself and others, just to crack a joke? What was he thinking?

"He's not an *idiot*," I told one of them.

"But he was in that instance," came the reply.

Others guessed that at the crucial juncture of sending the box, Snowden may have felt like he was on what amounted to a suicide mission. Dale and I hoped to answer this question — and maybe a good many others — by talking to Snowden himself. We were optimistic because, even in exile, Snowden granted tons of interviews. He spoke with everyone from Brian Lehrer and John Oliver to Katie Couric and Oliver Stone. He collaborated with French electronica icon Jean-Michel Jarre on the music video for a jittery techno track called "Exit."

Snowden was even a headliner for a positive-psychology seminar called Get Motivated!, which is famous for peddling get-rich-quick schemes to huge audiences at megachurches and arenas. ("This memorable ONE DAY seminar will give you proven strategies to sharpen your business skills, ignite your motivation, increase your effectiveness and multiply your income!" boasted the event's website, which also promised "incredible pyrotechnics, live music and spectacular special effects.")

While researching the magazine article that led to this book, Dale and I decided to seek an audience with the man in Moscow. Several of Snowden's confidants, including Laura, Micah Lee, and Ben Wizner, offered to help.

But his first response wasn't promising. "I'm not sure I'm ready to tell my side of that part of the timeline yet," Snowden replied. Later, Laura reached out again on our behalf. He emailed her:

I'll think about their request, but I'm doing much less media nowadays outside of obligations (like anniversaries).

It'll probably be a while before I'm excited about the idea of more interviews. I suspect you might know the feeling.

But what *was* Snowden feeling? Fatigue? Annoyance? Fear? There was no way to know. I reflected on the hell he'd surely been through, the dark residue of a trauma beyond imagining. I thought back to Laura's torturous months in Berlin, rereading the excerpts she had published from her journal. While waiting for Snowden to send the box, Laura had moved into a new apartment, in case her former location had somehow been compromised. She was alone and knew she could be arrested at any time. There was no word from Snowden. She was trapped in accelerating spiral of paranoia.

"I've created my own isolation, so they win," Laura wrote. "They always win. I can fight all I want and I will lose. I will be destroyed, paranoid, forsaken, unable to sleep, think, love."

That's not what happened, though. Instead of getting raided by police, she heard from Dale: the box was safe.

"The plans arrived, so I should have them tonight and begin distribution," she wrote in her final journal entries. "I should also destroy this fucking notebook."

She didn't destroy it, though. She seemed struck by the same documentarian's urge that Dale felt when he ignored her directions to burn Snowden's empty shipping box.

On October 10, 2014, Dale and I sat in the audience as the lights went down for the premiere of Laura's film *Citizenfour* at the New York Film Festival. The opening scene was shot from a car hurtling through a dark tunnel in Hong Kong. It was disorienting and claustrophobic, suffused with the same anxiety that had filled her journal. Nearly two hours later, we joined the standing ovation for what the

Guardian later described as "a triumph of journalism and a triumph for journalism." Four months later, *Citizenfour* would win an Oscar.

But for those of us who'd watched Laura navigate this saga from the start, the most powerful moment came after the screening. Laura took the stage, smiling exhaustedly, surrounded by the impromptu family that had bonded around her project. Investigative journalist Jeremy Scahill told the audience that Laura was "the most bad-ass director alive, period." Most moving was the tribute from the whistleblower's father, Lonnie Snowden, a retired Coast Guard officer.

"I would like to personally thank Laura and everyone for this wonderful piece of work," he told the crowd. "The truth is coming, and it cannot be stopped. I believe there's far more."

Laura had finally emerged from the long tunnel of making the film, an experience that seeped indelibly into her life. Around the same time, Dale and I began wondering: would fallout from the Snowden affair follow us into the future? Perhaps we'd just inhaled the equivalent of second-hand smoke from other people's paranoia, but we wanted to know: what, if anything, did the government have on file about us?

For years we'd kicked around the idea of sending Freedom of Information Act letters to the NSA and the FBI, asking for our files. In February and March 2018, we separately mailed our requests. Roughly two weeks later, we received matching rejection notices.

This was a paragraph from the NSA letter:

To respond to your request, NSA would have to confirm or deny the existence of intelligence records on you. Were we to do so in your case, we would have to do so for every other requester. This would enable, for example, a terrorist or other adversary to file a FOIA request with us in order to determine whether he or she was under surveillance or had evaded it. This in turn would allow that individual to better assess whether they could successfully act to damage the national security of the United States. For such reasons, we can neither confirm nor deny the existence or non-existence of the records you requested.

We were fascinated that all the rejections used some version of the same phrase: "we can neither confirm nor deny." This is what has come to be called a "Glomar" response. Nowadays, there are so many FOIA requests like ours that apparently an entire federal office is dedicated to processing similar rejections. People who get their requests denied have started referring to the rejection process as getting "Glomared."

The name "Glomar" comes from the *Hughes Glomar Explorer*, a ship the CIA used in the mid-1970s while trying salvage a sunken Soviet submarine. The CIA declined to "confirm or deny" the existence of the Glomar operation in response to a public records request from *Rolling Stone*. At the time, "neither confirm or deny" was a novel form of rejection. Invented as a legal tool for government officials to fend off the press, it was intended for use only in situations that posed dire threats to national security.

Laura also got Glomared when she requested her intelligence files. Attorneys from EFF later sued the US government to release them. When Laura finally received her FBI files, they'd been heavily redacted.

Not long after Dale and I got Glomared, Laura joined the two of us for dinner at my apartment. She knew we were still trying to make sense of what had happened since I received Snowden's box in 2013. That same year, she'd told Dale that we could visit her in Berlin to participate in the reporting — though Dale had still felt it wasn't his story and the message hadn't made it to me. (Frankly, I suspect I'd have jumped at the chance to be a part of that, and I'd always wanted to visit Berlin. Oh well!)

Now we described to Laura how the NSA and FBI had refused to turn over our files for this book. Perhaps, she suggested, we would like to have the experience of seeing what had come in the box — the Snowden archive — for our book?

At her suggestion, the next day we wrote a brief, formal request to the *Intercept*, the online news outlet she'd cofounded with Greenwald and Scahill in February 2014 to serve as an institutional home for reporting on the archive. the *Intercept* was published by First Look Media, a larger network of news platforms bankrolled by eBay founder Pierre Omidyar.

We were invited to report at the physical site that held the archive for two days in April. But three days before the scheduled visit, we received an unexpected email. First Look Media was asking us to sign an access agreement, stating the company would own all rights to any publication that resulted from our writing about the Snowden archive. It included a long section on confidentiality. We would be prohibited from writing about "any information relating to [First Look Media's] unpublished reporting, its sources, or its methods of newsgathering or its editorial procedures and policies." It also barred us from reporting "any information reflecting Collaborator's access or the extent of such access to the Snowden Archive."

We also learned that any notes we took at the archive would be confiscated for review — and possible redaction — by the *Intercept*.

With all those prohibitions, what would a pair of long-form journalists be able to write about? I sent an email describing the conundrum to David Bralow, an attorney at First Look Media. It read: "Unfortunately, the restrictions preclude our taking notes and describing anything about the experience of querying the archive — practices at the heart of narrative journalism, which is our craft."

If we signed the agreement, legally, this book would no longer have the right to exist. So we didn't. I called Laura. She was surprised. She told us that, when she'd approached Bralow and asked the *Intercept* to let us access the archive, she'd explained our role in the backstory. But the request was turned down anyway.

I laughed. The experience felt like something out of Kafka. And it gave me a sense of déjà vu, echoing how the NSA and the FBI had shut down our request to see our files.

Wasn't it kind of funny, I suggested, to get Glomared by the *Intercept*?

Meanwhile, Laura had been facing challenges of her own at the company, including the startling realization that her compensation was far below that of her male colleagues Greenwald and Scahill.

"I learned in 2016 that Glenn and Jeremy had renegotiated their contracts with management and there was a substantial pay disparity — hundreds of thousands of dollars," she explained. Her cofounders had received raises and bonuses from the company; as a result, Greenwald's pay had grown to more than double hers.

Laura filed a gender pay equity complaint with human resources. Negotiations followed; she was offered revised contracts with lower compensation and worse terms than those afforded Greenwald and Scahill, she said. When she refused to accept them, she added, she found herself excluded from senior-level decisions and meetings. In 2017, First Look Media CEO Michael Bloom offered her a buyout in exchange for leaving the company and signing a nondisclosure agreement. She refused and filed a retaliation complaint.

"It's very disappointing that an organization that claims to stand for whistleblower protection and accountability doesn't live up to those standards internally," she told us.

Meanwhile the Snowden archive's days at the *Intercept* were numbered. In March 2019, the company shut it down. Bloom wrote in a letter to staff that the *Intercept* had chosen to "focus on other editorial priorities." The company also laid off the research department that maintained the archive.

Neither Laura or Snowden had been consulted about the decision to defund the research team and shut down the archive.

In a letter to First Look's board of directors, Laura wrote, "This decision and the way it was handled would be a disservice to our source, the risks we've all taken, and most importantly, to the public for whom Edward Snowden blew the whistle."

She added that, even though the archive was no longer breaking news, "it remains the most significant historical archive documenting the rise of the surveillance state in the twenty-first century . . . I have advocated for years that we transition our approach to long-form books and historical research, formats that would maximize the historical impact of the archive not driven by the news cycle."

The day after the announcement, the *Intercept's* union invited Laura to attend a meeting where managers, along with Greenwald and Scahill, would take questions about all the cutbacks. As a cofounder of the *Intercept*, it only made sense for her to be there. But in a surprising snub, Bralow — the same First Look attorney we'd encountered earlier — barred her from attending. Four months later, things got weirder. First Look Media announced more layoffs. Rumors spread that the company was buying Passionflix, a website owned by Tosca Musk — Elon Musk's sister — that streams adaptations of romance novels. (Viewers are invited to rank the videos using a "barometer of naughtiness.")

Had management lost its collective mind? Dozens of employees wrote the board of directors, demanding to know what was going on. A *New York* magazine reporter asked First Look about Passionflix. Without addressing whether the two companies were — or had been — in talks, a spokesman said, "there is no deal to discuss at this point." (Months later, with very little public fanfare, the acquisition was finalized.)

We emailed Rodrigo Brandão, the *Intercept's* communications director, to ask for the company's perspective on all these matters. "Thanks for reaching out, but we cannot comment," he replied. We also sent two emails full of questions to Greenwald, who did not reply.

With First Look in disarray, the free press suffered an even greater blow that spring. In an eighteen-count indictment, the federal government accused Julian Assange of violating the Espionage Act by seeking out the classified information he published on WikiLeaks. Civil liberties advocates were alarmed by this latest attack on the First

Amendment by the Trump administration and worried about what it would mean for investigative news organizations and whistleblowers alike.

The indictment also singled out Jabber as part of the so-called conspiracy. This secure communications tool had been used by Assange and Manning — but also by Laura and Dale and countless of other journalists who were doing their jobs, working to protect confidential sources during investigative projects. The suggestion that encrypted messaging could be evidence of a conspiracy had an immediate chilling effect.

Micah Lee took to Twitter in protest.

"The indictment against Assange sets a dangerous precedent," he wrote. "If this sticks, what stops them from charging other journalists with 'conspiracy' for deleting metadata and chat logs to protect sources, encouraging sources to leak documents, or using whistleblower submission systems?"

Snowden chimed in, tweeting: "The Department of Justice just declared war — not on WikiLeaks, but on journalism itself. This is no longer about Julian Assange: This case will decide the future of media."

As we were finishing this book, Laura stepped down from her role as executive producer of First Look Media's documentary unit, Field of Vision, and was still trying to find a new home for the Snowden archive. She hoped it would land at a research institution, available to historians and longform journalists who see it as an object of cultural importance — not just a headline generator.

She kindly offered to let us sit with the archive too. By

this point, however, we'd come to feel that the focus of our book was the human relationships that shepherded Snowden's box — rather than the material inside. So we let it go.

So much had happened since the box arrived. Dale and I were driven by a desire for deeper understanding, a sense of what it all meant. As Snowden himself once put it: "Humans are by nature pattern-recognition machines. We search for meaning, whether in the circumstances of our lives or on the surface of toast."

Like Laura, we emerged from the dark tunnel of those tense years. We made peace knowing that there are questions we'll never be able to answer. We're only human, after all. We do what we can with the information we have. And we move on.

But the experience changed us. Even though the world is full of things we can't control, we do what we can. Just like I covered that godforsaken picnic table — over and over again — even though I knew it was a hapless pursuit. It means speaking out, telling human stories, even at the risk of being branded a co-conspirator.

To us, being alive means giving a damn. It means doing what we can to be useful during our time on this planet, even if our efforts amount to nothing. We know that privacy matters. We believe surveillance is corrosive to the human spirit — to creativity and openness and ultimately to our ability to love and trust one another.

When my family gave me an Amazon Echo and later, a Google Home, as well-meaning Christmas gifts, I quietly returned them. Dale and I put tape over our laptop cameras. We experimented with various platforms for encrypted messaging. We started using Signal and ProtonMail and got our editors to use them, too. We've tried to educate ourselves and others, spoken about the importance of privacy to our students and friends. (For links to some strong privacy tools and easy-to-use techniques, see the appendix at the end of this book.)

People who care about privacy aren't just protecting themselves, after all. They're part of a larger community. The more people who use encryption and other anti-surveillance tools, the harder it becomes for malevolent figures to track individuals — building a bigger haystack around a needle.

"We should all be sending encrypted cat pictures to each other," Laura told a group of journalists in Berlin in 2014. If everyone participated, she suggested, it would overwhelm the NSA's ability to monitor American citizens."

In other words: individual decisions matter. So often we're told they don't. That it's not worth taking action — voting, speaking out, even writing — because single people are so small, the world too big. Yet we persist.

We do it for the same reason that we choose trust over fear. Writing in the face of silence. Living despite the shadow of mortality. Caring for people even though it makes us vulnerable.

Though George Orwell is best known for the dark themes he explored in 1984, he is also a great humanist who wrote:

The essence of being human is that one does not seek perfection . . . that one does not push asceticism to the point where it makes friendly intercourse impossible, and that one is prepared in the end to be defeated and broken up by life, which is the inevitable price of fastening one's love upon other human individuals.

To this day, his words bring consolation. We are journalists and seekers, but the truth — the full truth — will always be elusive. That said, there's one thing I know for sure. If Dale had warned me in 2013 that receiving the box might be dangerous, I would have done it all over again for him. Friendship is like that.

The Box

We used to look back with dread on the days immediately following the Snowden leaks. Over time, those memories softened around the edges, coming to feel like a long, strange dream. The tense moments were tempered by gentler days that followed — in particular, one blue-sky summer afternoon at Dale's off-grid home in California.

More than three years had passed since Dale had cached a copy of the Snowden material in a Douglas fir. For a brief window of time, we weren't preoccupied with worry. Assange hadn't been indicted yet. It appeared that Laura and the other players were safe. Snowden seemed to be settling into his new home in Moscow, where he'd been joined by his partner, Lindsay Mills.

We walked across Prosper Ridge, where the home Dale had built nestled into an embankment below a vast, grassy meadow. There were no helicopters buzzing overhead. No need to hide cellphones in a fridge.

We approached the place where Snowden's material was hidden and propped the ladder against the ancient tree. Then one of us made a joke: what if the material was gone? Suddenly, the day didn't seem so sunny in the deep shade of the forest.

We took turns holding the ladder and climbing. Once we reached the top, it was easy to continue higher, going from branch to branch, up to where the material was located. A bird had built a nest on top of the sealed container. Happily, that nest was empty: breeding season had passed. We opened the container. The material was inside.

We lingered in the tree, taking in a panoramic view of the Pacific — along with the sound of distant waves crashing and the sharp scent of fir sap. We could see the studio where Laura worked on her mini-documentary about William Binney, the film Snowden cited as a reason for contacting her in the first place. In a sense, we were back where our bit part in the Snowden narrative had begun. It felt good to pause and rest before we climbed back to earth.

We brought the material down so it could be moved elsewhere. Why keep it at all? There's always the possibility it could be seized as evidence, especially given the zealousness of the Trump administration, the paranoid fantasy that journalists are all players in some vast conspiracy.

Yet we hang on to such items. The box and the copies of what it contained are artifacts of a critical moment in American history, especially for anyone who cares about the Fourth Amendment and government abuse of power. They've also become part of our lives, another chapter in a long and ongoing friendship.

Maybe it's human nature to focus on the tension and emotion from the summer of 2013. We're reliving it now, just by telling this story. But when we look at the pictures we took as we climbed down from the tree, in most of them, we're smiling.

APPENDIX

Sanity in the Age of Surveillance

Now that surveillance is everywhere, what can people do to protect themselves?

If you've read this far, you've already taken the first step: caring about the impact of mass spying on an open society. If you feel moved to act, there are concrete steps you can follow to defend your privacy.

The first thing to do is assess your personal risk profile. What kind of information are you trying to secure? Whom are you trying to keep it from — advertisers, scammers, corporations, the government? What's the worst thing that can happen if it leaks out? And what kind of trade-offs are you willing to make to protect it?

Let's assume you're a civilian. You don't anticipate receiving an archive of classified NSA files in the mail. But you also don't want to get hacked, and you dislike the idea of companies and law enforcement agencies having a one-way window into your personal life. (To reiterate the example raised by John Oliver's correspondent: you don't want feds ogling your "dick pics.")

We believe that privacy — like food, water, and shelter — is a human right worth defending. But before you think globally, consider acting locally: with yourself. You don't need to be a cyberninja to use encryption for everyday messaging.

As of this writing, Signal remains one of the simplest — and most secure — messaging apps available. It's great for sending texts but also encrypts voice and video calls, documents, and images. Developed by the nonprofit OpenWhisper Systems, Signal is free, community-supported, peer-reviewed open-source software that wins raves from security researchers and privacy advocates. After Trump won the 2016 US election, Signal downloads jumped by 400 percent in the span of a month, according to Moxie Marlinspike, the app's creator.

"Trump has threatened a lot of people and he's about to be in control of the most pervasive and least accountable surveillance infrastructure in the world," Marlinspike told the *New York Times*. "A lot of people are justifiably concerned about that."

Another reasonable choice for secure messaging is WhatsApp, which uses the same end-to-end encryption technology that Marlinspike developed for Signal and boasts more than 1.5 billion users worldwide. However, WhatsApp was acquired for $19 billion by Facebook in 2014, which means some privacy advocates distrust it on principle. And unlike Signal, it stores decrypted backups of your messages on your phone and, depending on how you've configured your settings, possibly on iCloud or Google Drive. So while your messages should be safe in transit, they're still vulnerable after reaching their destination.

As we were completing this book, an international cabal of government officials — US attorney general William P. Barr,

UK home secretary Priti Patel, acting US homeland security secretary Kevin McAleenan, and Australian minister for home affairs Peter Dutton — had begun pressuring Facebook to create a back door in WhatsApp and its other messaging services that would allow law enforcement agencies to spy on users' private communications.

"Companies should not deliberately design their systems to preclude any form of access to content even for preventing or investigating the most serious crimes," they wrote in a letter to Mark Zuckerberg.

Facebook fired back. "End-to-end encryption already protects the messages of over a billion people every day," Andy Stone, a company spokesman, told the *New York Times*. "We strongly oppose government attempts to build backdoors because they would undermine the privacy and security of people everywhere."

Weeks later, Facebook sued NSO Security, an Israeli company, claiming it had hacked WhatsApp servers in an effort to access private correspondence from journalists, diplomats, human rights activists, and government officials by planting malware on some 1,400 mobile phones.

If you use WhatsApp and value your ability to communicate confidentially, it's worth following these matters closely.

If you're already using secure text messaging and want to go further, consider setting up encrypted email. As of this writing, one of the easiest options is ProtonMail, a free, open-source provider based in Switzerland with end-to-end encryption. It doesn't offer all the bells and whistles found on commercial services like Gmail, Outlook, and YahooMail, but we've both found it tremendously useful as a secure, use-as-needed secondary account. (When we started writing the magazine article that led to this book, we convinced our *Harper's* editor, James Marcus, to get a ProtonMail account too.)

The service does have drawbacks: its end-to-end encryption only works if you're emailing another ProtonMail user. The main benefit is that your messages remain encrypted on ProtonMail's server. If government officials demanded to see a copy of your correspondence, all ProtonMail would be able to provide them is metadata, including subject lines. The content of the messages would remain in code.

If you want more robust protection — and you're ready to engage a higher level of complexity — consider taking a deep dive into PGP-encrypted email. The website OpenPGP (www. openpgp.org) lists a range of software to get you up and running, including the popular Gpg4win for Windows and GPGTools for Mac.

And if you're a whistleblower, it's worth remembering: snail mail remains among the best ways to leak material to a journalist. In the summer of 2019, the *New York Times* received a brown envelope containing almost a hundred pages of sealed court and other documents that revealed possible medical malpractice in the death of Neil Armstrong, the first human on the moon.

Even if you don't foresee a need for encrypted communications, it's worth making sure online predators aren't using email as a phishing rod into your life. Avoid following links and opening files from untrusted senders. If you must open a suspicious attachment, experts recommend that you do it in Google Docs, so any infections don't end up on your computer.

As a prophylactic, consider installing anti-malware

software — such as MalwareBytes, which is free — and set it up to scan your machine regularly.

If you want to browse the internet without Big Brother as your copilot, consider trying Tor Browser, which routes your online navigation through a network of encrypted relays. Tor doesn't play nice with advertisers, blocking background scripts and the browser-tracking technologies that follow your every move. When you log off, your browsing history gets wiped out. The downside? All these features make Tor run a bit more slowly than commercial browsers.

Firefox and Safari are also catching up to consumers' demands for privacy, integrating anti-tracking features and preferences into their software.

No matter what browser you use, it's worth remembering: Google and other commercial search engines act like giant vacuum cleaners, hoovering up your queries as an endless stream of market research. Their algorithms deliver results based on what they think you want, creating the kind of echo chamber technologists call a "filter bubble." If you don't want your searches tracked, try a private browser like DuckDuckGo — and note how different the results are.

Some privacy-minded folks take one extra step, using a VPN — virtual private network — that camouflages online traffic. VPNs are services — some free, some subscription-based — which raises a whole new set of issues around trust and vulnerability. In 2006, the NSA cracked the VPNs used by Al Jazeera, the Iraqi military, and Russian airlines and other targets. We know that thanks to the Snowden archive.

It's also worth securing your online accounts, which are only as robust as the passwords protecting them. With data breaches happening all the time, even the strongest passwords can be compromised in an instant.

Unless you're really good at memorizing long strings of gibberish — or have an affinity for Post-It notes — consider seeking professional help. Password managers like LastPass and 1Password can help you generate strong passwords, keep them in order, and notify you if any of your login credentials have been compromised in a data breach. (If you're curious to see whether your individual accounts have been hacked, you can also spot-check them at this handy — and scary — website: www.haveibeenpwned.com.)

And don't forget to consider the obvious: that ubiquitous, selfie-taking orifice on your laptop or smartphone. To keep your camera working for you — and away from voyeurs — it's worth slapping a removable cover on it. Even Zuckerberg — who knows a thing or two about violating privacy — does it. Electrical or duct tape will do. EFF also sells some cute stickers on its website. They're easy to peel off and support a good cause, too.

Take a Marie Kondo approach to your digital life. Unsubscribe from old mailing lists that no longer spark joy. Purge computer and smartphone apps you don't use anymore. Remember that apps can run in the background of your devices. Even when you're not actively using them, they may be using you — as a valuable source of free data.

If you're a Mac user, try experimenting with Little Snitch, free software that monitors your network traffic, detecting outbound connections from various apps. Similar applications are available for Windows too. Sometimes, you may find that your computer has been having a party without you.

Do an audit of your house. Do you use networked appliances: security devices such as doorbell cameras or so-called "smart" speakers, televisions, or thermostats? These gizmos add comfort to our lives, but they also stalk us relentlessly — both online and in the physical world, often without our consciously consenting to this digital home invasion. Read the fine print. Decide how much of your privacy you're willing to sacrifice in the name of convenience.

Keep in mind that the burgeoning field of digital forensics has turned its attention to the internet of things. Nowadays, there are entire college programs dedicated to mining the data gathered by our digital devices.

Carry this approach over to social media. Facebook, Twitter, Instagram, and other platforms may keep you virtually connected with friends and family. Their primary purpose, however, is mapping your patterns of consumption and even your political preferences, which may be sold to the highest bidder. When you tag friends in a photo, you're also adding their faces to a massive biometric database. In other words: social media is *not* the place to dance like no one's watching.

If you're an activist or a citizen journalist, consider building a toolkit that supports your work in the field.

At protests or political events, consider stashing your cellphone in a simple Faraday bag that blocks it from sending or receiving signals. (As of this writing, they're available online for about $11 apiece.) This might seem like the modern-day equivalent of wearing a tinfoil hat, but it's not — police have tracked cell signals at Occupy Wall Street and other civic demonstrations to identify the people who are participating.

Security researchers also urge citizen journalists to back up their footage to a trusted space in the cloud, in case their devices are confiscated. The American Civil Liberties Union maintains a tool called the Mobile Justice App, which allows smartphone users to transmit video directly to the organization. As of this writing, it's available in eighteen states, including Arizona, California, Michigan, and New Jersey, and the District of Columbia.

Even if the feds can't track your phone, they've likely got your face in a database. But facial recognition is problematic for a slew of reasons. Beyond those we've already discussed, the algorithms are strongly biased towards white men and are much more likely to misidentify women and people of color — amplifying preexisting racial and gender biases. Enter Hyphen-Labs, an international collective of women technologists of color. The group is working with Berlin artist and privacy advocate Adam Harvey on the HyperFace Project: a purple camouflage scarf packed with ghost faces, designed to scramble computer-vision algorithms.

In the meantime, Harvey has also been developing CV Dazzle: a free toolkit of fashion-based strategies that use hair and makeup to thwart facial-recognition software. The name is an homage to Dazzle camouflage — also known as Razzle Dazzle — a series of striking, black-and-white patterns used by the Allies during World War I to conceal their battleships' size and orientation.

Automated license-plate readers are also an insidious tool used by law enforcement agencies to track how we travel. In response, companies have started selling spray coatings that render plates' digits invisible to cameras on the highway. The artist and activist Kate Bertash also offers a stylish alternative: T-shirts printed with a scramble of license plates to confound the algorithms. They are available for about $40 apiece at her website, which also includes a guide on how you can make your own.

Stay Informed

Technologies evolve — and new tools emerge — over time. Some of the best clearinghouses for current information include the Electronic Frontier Foundation's Surveillance Self-Defense website and the EPIC Online Guide to Practical Privacy Tools, hosted by the Electronic Privacy Information Center.

And it's worth keeping an eye on surveillance law. In 2018, the European Union passed the General Data Protection Regulation (GDPR), which slaps companies with substantial fines for invading privacy. Internet users must opt in to have their data shared, and, as a result, Europeans should experience far fewer tracking ads.

Brazil, Japan, and South Korea immediately began following Europe's lead with this law. "If we can export this to the world, I will be happy," Vera Jourova told the *New York Times*. Jourova, who helped draft the regulation, is the European commissioner for justice, consumers, and gender equality.

While the United States largely lags behind, the ACLU has pushed for greater oversight of domestic spying in America. In 2016, it launched an initiative called Community Control Over Police Surveillance, with the goal of helping citizens lobby for local legislation regulating law enforcement's ability to eavesdrop.

A dozen jurisdictions, from the city of Seattle to the Bay

Area Rapid Transit system, have adopted CCOPS laws. Some thirty other cities have movements to push for these controls.

The state that gave us Silicon Valley is also leading the way to regulate what the tech bros wrought. California passed a law, due to take effect this year, allowing consumers to force companies to delete — and not sell — their personal data. In 2018, San Francisco passed the "Stop Secret Surveillance" ordinance, which bans any city agencies from using facial recognition technology. The following year, Oakland adopted a similar ban.

Getting Involved

In the absence of regulatory oversight, a number of nonprofit and nongovernmental organizations around the world have taken the lead in defending people against government surveillance and insidious corporate eavesdropping. Joining or donating to such groups is a great way to further their efforts.

In the United States, the Electronic Frontier Foundation is a pioneer. The organization was founded in San Francisco in 1990 to promote and protect civil liberties on the rapidly evolving internet. As the digital world has grown, so has EFF, which actively monitors policy, fights legal battles in court, and organizes political action on behalf of human rights.

In the United Kingdom, the nonprofit Privacy International initiates lawsuits and public pressure campaigns, working on issues that range from personal data protection to fighting what it refers to as "government hacking powers." In 2018, the group filed complaints against data brokers and credit agencies, including Equifax, with the independent regulatory office that monitors the European Union's General Data Protection Regulation.

Amnesty International is another heavy hitter in the arena of privacy protection. In a 2016 study called "For Your Eyes Only? Ranking 11 Technology Companies on Encryption and Human Rights," Amnesty's researchers found that many major firms are failing to provide their users with a reasonable standard of security. Their report noted that "only three of the companies assessed — Apple, LINE, Viber Media — apply end-to-end encryption as a default to all of their IM services. Of these, none are fully transparent about the system of encryption they are using." The researchers also learned that some companies don't practice what they preach. "For example, Microsoft has a clear stated commitment to human rights, but is not applying any form of end-to-end encryption on its Skype service," they wrote.

Other organizations are leading the charge to protect the rights of minorities and targeted groups. All Out, a global LGBT+ rights organization, has mobilized members to protest what it has referred to as the Egyptian government's "anti-gay witch hunt": the surveillance and arrest of gay, bi, and trans Egyptians. The Center for Constitutional Rights has long fought against government surveillance, beginning not long after the Cointelpro operations were exposed. In the wake of 9/11, the center challenged local police departments' overzealous surveillance of Muslim communities and federal agencies' efforts to have Muslims spy on their own communities.

The center also partnered with a newer civil rights group, Color of Change, to file a Freedom of Information Act request with the FBI and the US Department of Homeland Security, demanding documentation of how the government monitored Black Lives Matter activists. In the fall of 2019, Color of Change, which boasts some 1.4 million members, won a major victory when Google booted payday lenders — notorious for targeting low-income Americans with high-interest, predatory financial products — from its app store.

And the ACLU, a century old in 2020, continues to add to its storied history of shining a light on institutions that abuse the public trust. In 2018, it helped expose overreach by the home security company Ring, acquired by Amazon that year for between $1.2 and $1.8 billion. Ring has partnered with more than 225 police agencies around the United States — often bolstered by taxpayer dollars — to either give away or sell the company's "smart" doorbell cameras, which law enforcement officers can then use as a distributed surveillance network. The Massachusetts ACLU said it was filing one hundred public records requests regarding possible Ring contracts with police departments in the state.

This patchwork of allied organizations might seem small now, but it is growing daily, even as we finish this book. Most recently, the consumer interest group Public Citizen — founded in 1971, and now with 500,000 members — was featured in a *New York Times* op-ed by Natasha Singer, who called for increased federal oversight of apps and smart technology, noting that "the United States is virtually the only developed nation without a comprehensive consumer data protection law and an independent agency to enforce it."

"Independent" is the most important word in the preceding sentence. If the United States were to create such an entity, its mission would be twofold: protecting citizens from both the corporations that monetize our data and the law enforcement agencies they collude with under the banner of surveillance capitalism.

This may sound like a terribly remote hope. Given the state of political turmoil in the United States, it's a dream that could easily sound naive. But we refuse to submit to cynicism. If a ragtag band of concerned citizens could shepherd Snowden's secrets from the darkness onto the front pages of international newspapers, it's worth asking yourself: what can I do? Better yet: what can we do together?

Acknowledgments

This is, at heart, a book about some of the most powerful analog technology in the world: human relationships. (To us, the project has always felt like a buddy movie; Jess ended up nicknaming it "Harold and Kumar Go to the NSA.")

Of course, a project like this couldn't happen without a posse, and we're in debt to everyone who threw down/showed up/helped out.

First, we'd like to thank our dear friend James Marcus, who edited the original incarnation of this story for *Harper's Magazine*.

We'd also like to thank Andrew Hsiao, our ever-patient editor at Verso, along with Joy Harris and Adam Reed at the Joy Harris Literary Agency.

We're grateful to everyone who made time to speak with us, including Ben Wizner at the ACLU and Trevor Timm at the Freedom of the Press Foundation. Micah Lee was a techno-mensch — our PGP Virgil — and we hope he'll invite us to another *Mr. Robot* watch party someday. Kirsten Johnson let us see the world through her lens — with warmth, humor, and openness.

This book would not exist without Laura Poitras, aka "the Chef," who got us into this mess and had the forbearance to see us through to the other side. We're grateful for her participation as a source, a reader, and, above all, a friend.

We'd also like to thank Julia Moburg and Ron Bruder, who were thoughtful readers, confidants, and integral to the barn-raising effort.

We'd like to thank the Corporation of Yaddo and the MacDowell Colony, where parts of this book were written.

And, of course, we'd like to thank Max the spaniel, who has offered unconditional affection since the beginning and keeps secrets better than anyone. We sure wish he could read.

Notes

Some of the reporting in this book first appeared in "Snowden's Box: The Human Network behind the Biggest Leak of All," an article we coauthored for the May 2017 *Harper's Magazine*.

We conducted interviews from 2016 to 2019 with Barton Gellman, Micah Lee, Kirsten Johnson, Laura Poitras, Trevor Timm, Ben Wizner, and confidential sources.

Foreword

p. 2 **The cover of the Guardian bore a giant yellow headline:** Julian Borger and Glenn Greenwald, "The Whistleblower" *Guardian,* October 6, 2013.

p. 2 **Snowden's trademark eyeglasses:** James Bamford, "The Most Wanted Man In The World," *Wired*, September 2014.

p. 2 **an existential threat to democracy:** Glenn Greenwald, Ewen MacAskill, and Laura Poitras, "Edward Snowden: The Whistleblower behind the NSA Surveillance Revelations,"

Guardian, June 9, 2013.

p. 3   **General Social Survey:** Chris Cillizza, "Watch Americans' Trust in Each Other Erode over the Last Four Decades," *Washington Post*, May 31, 2014; Josh Morgan, "The Decline of Trust in the United States: A Look at the Trend and What Can Be Done About It," *Medium*, May 20, 2014; "Can People Be Trusted," GSS Data Explorer, https://gssdataexplorer.norc.org/variables/441/vshow.

p. 4   **most notorious surveillance state in modern history:** Mary Williams Walsh, "Germans Debate Sins of the Past," *Los Angeles Times*, March 2, 1995; Deutsche Presse-Agentur, "Spying Activity Detailed: East German Agency Had Huge Network, Committee Reports," *Hartford Courant*, September 9, 1990.

pp. 4–5   **even in systems with fewer informants:** For comparison, the official head count of the NSA is around 35,000. Scott Shane and Jo Becker, "N.S.A. Appears to Have Missed 'Big Red Flags' in Suspect's Behavior," *New York Times*, October 30, 2016.

p. 5   **Clive Norris testimony before members of British Parliament:** "Surveillance: Citizens and the State," Constitution Committee, House of Lords, November 28, 2007, https://publications.parliament.uk/pa/ld200809/ldselect/ldconst/18/7112804.htm.

p. 5   **one of the most extensive surveillance systems in the world:** Harriet Agerholm, "UK Mass Surveillance Programme Violates Human Rights, European Court Rules," *Independent*, September 13, 2018.

p. 5   **"fosters suspicion," undermines "cohesion and solidarity" and amounts to "a slow social suicide":** David Lyon et al., *A Report on the Surveillance Society*, "for the Information

Commissioner by the Surveillance Studies Network" (Information Commissioner's Office, 2006), https://ico.org. uk/media/about-the-ico/documents/1042390/surveil-lance-society-full-report-2006.pdf.

p. 5 **"peak indifference":** Cory Doctorow, "We Cannot Afford to Be Indifferent to Internet Spying," *Guardian*, December 9, 2013.

pp. 5–6 **Clipper chip:** Andi Wilson Thompson, Danielle Kehl, and Kevin Bankston, "Doomed to Repeat History? Lessons from the Crypto Wars of the 1990s," New America, June 17, 2015, https://newamerica.org/; Steven Levy, "The Battle of the Clipper Chip," *New York Times Magazine*, June 12, 1994; Philip Elmer-Dewitt, "Who Should Keep the Keys?" *Time*, March 14, 1994; Stewart A. Baker, "Don't Worry Be Happy: Why Clipper Is Good for You," *Wired*, May 1994.

For a more appropriate soundtrack to government intrusion, try "Be Worry, Don't Happy," Oleg Berg's minor-key transposition of the Bobby McFerrin classic: youtube.com/watch?v=LbTxfN8d2CI.

p. 7 **Despite my intentions, I never created the time:** Glenn Greenwald, *No Place to Hide: Edward Snowden, the NSA and the Surveillance State* (New York: Metropolitan Books, 2014), 9.

p. 8 **You always have to trust somebody:** Jon Evans, "WhatsApp, Signal and Dangerously Ignorant Journalism," *TechCrunch*, January 22, 2017.

p. 9 **When his bad-faith testimony was exposed:** Andrew Rosenthal, "Making Alberto Gonzales Look Good," *New York Times*, June 11, 2013.

p. 9 **He assured Americans: a hunt was on:** "DNI's Clapper: Leaker Chose to 'Violate a Sacred Trust,'" NBC News, June

10, 2013, https://www.nbcnews.com/nightly-news/video/ dnis-clapper-leaker-chose-to-violate-a-sacred-trust-33011267943.

p. 9 **"clearly erroneous":** Spencer Ackerman, "Clapper: I Gave 'Erroneous' Answer Because I Forgot about Patriot Act," *Guardian*, July 2, 2013.

p. 10 **Trump is pushing to restore the NSA's access:** Charlie Savage, "Trump Administration Asks Congress to Reauthorize N.S.A.'s Deactivated Call Records Program," *New York Times*, August 15, 2019.

1. Winter Nights

p. 15 **"roving bug":** Declan McCullagh, "FBI Taps Cell Phone Mic as Eavesdropping Tool," CNET, December 4, 2006, Cnet.com; Kevin Coughlin, "Even if They're Off, Cell Phones Allow FBI to Listen In," *Seattle Times*, December 13, 2006.

p. 15 **"no credible evidence":** Jamie Williams and Karen Gullo, "Government Documents Show FBI Cleared Filmmaker Laura Poitras after Six-Year Fishing Expedition," Electronic Frontier Foundation, December 6, 2017, Eff.org.

p. 16 **she offered to write with crayons:** Peter Maass, "How Laura Poitras Helped Snowden Spill His Secrets," *New York Times Magazine*, August 18, 2013. Substantiated in interviews with Laura Poitras.

p. 17 *Salon* **ran an article:** Glenn Greenwald, "US Filmmaker Repeatedly Detained at Border," *Salon*, April, 8, 2012.

p. 18 **Laura was editing** *The Program***:** Laura Poitras, "The Program," *New York Times Op-Docs*, video, Nytimes.com; Paul Harris, "US Data Whistleblower: 'It's a Violation of Everybody's

Constitutional Rights,'" *Guardian*, September 15, 2012.

pp. 19–20 **According to the journalist James Bamford:** James Bamford, "The NSA Is Building the Country's Biggest Spy Center (Watch What You Say)," *Wired,* March 2012.

p. 27 **Magic Grow sponge-capsule safari animals:** Mom Knows Toys, "Magic Grow Capsules Safari Animals," YouTube, March 14, 2016, YouTube.

p. 29 **US Department of Justice had secretly seized records**: "Gov't Obtains Wide AP Phone Records in Probe," Associated Press, May 13, 2013, Ap.org.

p. 29 **federal investigators had also seized personal email and phone records:** Ann E. Marimow, "A Rare Peek into a Justice Department Leak Probe," *Washington Post,* May 19, 2013.

2. The Brittle Summer

p. 31 **Your worst enemy:** George Orwell, *1984* (London: Secker and Warburg, 1949), 81.

p. 31 **excerpts from Laura's Berlin journal:** Laura Poitras, *Astro Noise: A Survival Guide for Living under Total Surveillance* (Whitney Museum of American Art, 2016), 87, 89, 91, 95.

p. 33 **NSA considered Tails a "major" threat to intelligence gathering**: SIGDEV Conference 2012, "Making Things Measurable: Technology Trending Challenges and Approaches," June 2012, www.spiegel.de/media/media-35535.pdf, 20. See also "Inside the NSA's War on Internet Security," *Spiegel Online*.

p. 35 **The black budget mapped out $52.6 billion in spending on top-secret projects:** Barton Gellman and Greg Miller, "'Black Budget' Summary Details US Spy Network's Successes,

Failures and Objectives," *Washington Post*, August 29, 2013.

pp. 35–6   **poetic letter**: Greenwald, *No Place to Hide*, 31–32.

p. 36   **For a year and a half my greatest fear:** Daniel Ellsberg, *Secrets: A Memoir of Vietnam and the Pentagon Papers* (New York: Viking, 2002), 370.

p. 38   **They'd already met face-to-face in April**: Greenwald, *No Place to Hide*, 11.

p. 39   **The package was held up in customs for ten days:** Greenwald, *No Place to Hide*, 14.

p. 39   **My personal desire is that you paint the target directly on my back:** Laura Poitras, director, *Citizenfour* (RADiUS TWC/Participant Media, 2017), 19:30–20:00.

p. 40   **Approaching the *New York Times*, however, was out of the question:** David Folkenflick, "New York Times' Editor: Losing Snowden Scoop 'Really Painful,'" National Public Radio, June 5, 2014, Npr.org.

p. 40   ***New York Times* "far too accommodating of power":** Edward Snowden, encrypted email to Laura Poitras in early May 2013.

p. 40   **the *Times* spiked a story:** Margaret Sullivan, "Lessons in a Surveillance Drama Redux," *New York Times*, November 9, 2013.

p. 40   **which went on to win a Pulitzer Prize:** "James Risen and Eric Lichtblau of *The New York Times*," Pulitzer.org.

p. 41   **Gellman had his first direct exchange with Snowden:** Barton Gellman, "Code Name 'Verax': Snowden, in Exchanges with Post Reporter, Made Clear He Knew Risks," *Washington Post*, June 9, 2013.

pp. 41–6 **Laura and Greenwald travel to Hong Kong:** Greenwald, *No Place to Hide*, 24–33.

p. 42   **Espionage Act used more under Obama:** James Risen, "If

Donald Trump Targets Journalists, Thank Obama," *New York Times*, December 30, 2016.

p. 46 **ordered Verizon to turn over millions of US citizens' phone records:** "Verizon Forced to Hand over Telephone Data—Full Court Ruling," *Guardian*, June 5, 2013.

p. 47 **Six years earlier Obama had promised to end "the illegal wiretapping of American citizens":** "Obama Defends Surveillance Programs," *New York Times*, video, June 7, 2013, Nytimes.com.

p. 47 **Obama had also denounced the excesses of the so-called war on terror:** Maureen Dowd, "Peeping Barry," *New York Times*, June 6, 2019.

p. 47 **modest encroachments:** "Obama's Remarks on Health Care and Surveillance," *New York Times,* June 8, 2013.

p. 47 **Romero: "A pox on all the three houses of government":** Charlie Savage, Edward Wyatt, and Peter Baker, "US Confirms that It Gathers Online Data Overseas," *New York Times*, June 6, 2013.

p. 47 **overbroad interpretation of the Patriot Act:** Ellen Nakashima, Jerry Markon, Ed O'Keefe, "Lawmakers Defend and Criticize NSA Program to Collect Phone Logs," *Washington Post,* June 6, 2013.

p. 48 **the NSA had been collecting users' private communications:** Glenn Greenwald and Ewen MacAskill, "NSA Prism Program Taps in to User Data of Apple, Google and Others," *Guardian*, June 7, 2013; Barton Gelman and Laura Poitras, "US, British Intelligence Mining Data from Nine US Internet Companies in Broad Secret Program," *Washington Post*, June 7, 2013.

p. 48 **Snowden answering questions:** On June 9, the *Guardian* ran a short film by Laura Poitras. It showed Snowden answering questions posed by Greenwald. "NSA Whistleblower Edward Snowden: 'I don't want to live in a society that does these sort of things,'" *Guardian*, video, June 9, 2013, www.theguardian.com/world/video/2013/jun/09/nsa-whistleblower-edward-snowden-interview-video.

p. 48 **The Mira Hotel in Kowloon:** Ewen MacAskill, "Edward Snowden: How the Spy Story of the Age Leaked Out," *Guardian*, June 12, 2013.

p. 49 **"I will never commit suicide" (Binney):** Laura Poitras, *Astro Noise: A Survival Guide for Living under Total Surveillance* (New York: Whitney Museum of American Art, 2016), 100.

pp. 49–50 *The Program* **(Binney):** ibid.

p. 52 **Franklin D. Roosevelt:** In Samuel Rosenman, ed., *The Public Papers of Franklin D. Roosevelt*, vol. 2, *The Year of Crisis, 1933* (New York: Random House, 1938), 11–16.

p. 54 **Shane Miller:** Hector Becerra, "Man Allegedly Kills Family—and Then Disappears," *Los Angeles Times*, June 2, 2013.

p. 56 **federal officials charged him with espionage:** "Inside the NSA's War on Internet Security," *Spiegel Online*.

p. 56 **US government had bungled it:** Chester Yung and Te-Ping Chen, "Name Mix-Up Helped Snowden Leave Hong Kong," *Wall Street Journal*, June 26, 2013.

p. 56 **Boarded plane with Sarah Harrison:** Sara Corbett, "How a Snowdenista Kept the NSA Leaker Hidden in a Moscow Airport," *Vogue*, February 19, 2015.

pp. 56–7 **US Postal Service photographing and logging every single piece of mail:** Ron Nixon, "US Postal Service Logging All Mail for Law Enforcement," *New York Times,* July 3, 2013.

p. 57 **Jimmy Carter uses snail mail:** Andrea Mitchell, "A Call to Action: An Exclusive with Jimmy Carter," *Meet the Press*, NBC News, March 23, 2014.

p. 57 **surprise in mailbox**: Susanne Craig, "The Time I Found Donald Trump's Tax Records in My Mailbox," *New York Times*, October 2, 2016.

p. 59 **Massachusetts drug dealer busted after shipments tracked:** Jordan Pearson, "An Alleged Drug Dealer Got Busted by an IP Address and a Fake Mailman," *Vice*, May 12, 2015.

3. The Players

pp. 63–4 **Kirsten Johnson collaboration with Poitras:** Neta Alexander, "Filming Death and Living to Tell the Tale: Interview with Documentarian Kirsten Johnson," *Haaretz*, November 19, 2016.

p. 64 *The Oath*. Laura Poitras, director, *The Oath* (Zeitgeist Films, 2010).

p. 65 **Micah Lee and his wife in Berkeley**: Micah Lee, "Ed Snowden Taught Me to Smuggle Secrets Past Incredible Danger. Now I Teach You," *Intercept*, October 28, 2014.

p. 67 **Micah EFF start date:** Micah Lee, "Leaving EFF and Joining a Fearless Team of Journalists," Micah Lee's blog, November 15, 2013, micahflee.com.

p. 67 **Trevor EFF start date:** Trevor Timm, Linkedin, www.linkedin.com/in/trevor-timm-54346139.

p. 67 **WikiLeaks accounts frozen:** Robert Mackey, "PayPal Suspends WikiLeaks Account," The Lede, *New York Times*, December 4, 2010; Declan McCullagh, CBS News, December 6, 2010; "MasterCard Pulls Plug on WikiLeaks Payments," December 6, 2010; "WikiLeaks' Visa Payments Suspended," BBC News, December 7, 2010.

p. 67 **what EFF called an "economic blockade":** Shari Steele, "Join EFF in Standing Up against Internet Censorship," Electronic Frontier Foundation, December 7, 2010, Eff.org;

Cindy Cohn, "EFF Helps Freedom of the Press Foundation," Electronic Frontier Foundation, December 17, 2012, Eff.org.

p. 67 **Freedom of the Press Foundation's first website**: staff directory, https://web.archive.org/eb/20121218123732/ https://pressfreedomfoundation.org/about/staff.

p. 69 **inscrutable string of nonsense**: From an undated encrypted exchange between Laura Poitras and Dale Maharidge, circa summer or fall 2013.

p. 70 **sequence of events Micah would later recount**: Lee, "Ed Snowden Taught Me to Smuggle Secrets."

p. 70 **mysterious source had contacted another Freedom of the Press Foundation board member**: Greenwald, *No Place to Hide*, 7.

pp. 70–2 **twelve-minute instructional video**: anon108 [Edward Snowden], "GPG for Journalists," uploaded Sunday, January 6, 2013, vimeo.com/user15675314.

p. 72 **"Cincinnatus" described his mounting frustration**: Greenwald, *No Place to Hide*, 10.

p. 72 **Snowden had seen *The Program* and read what Greenwald had written about her in *Salon***: Maass, "How Laura Poitras Helped Snowden Spill His Secrets."

pp. 72–3 **"The surveillance you've experienced means you've been selected"**: Poitras, *Citizenfour*, 4:22–5:06.

p. 73 **DARKDIAMOND for Laura and SILVERSHOT for Micah**: Poitras, *Astro Noise*, 101.

p. 73 **COPPERCOMET for Greenwald**: Edward Snowden to Laura Poitras in an encrypted email on April 21, 2013.

pp. 73–4 **Henk Penning on trust**: "On the Apache.org Web of Trust," WebCite, webcitation.org.

p. 76 **"Whatever they were doing was sensitive"**: Lee, "Ed Snowden Taught Me to Smuggle Secrets."

pp. 76–7 **"confirm that no one has ever had a copy of your private key":** Poitras, *Citizenfour*, 1:19–1:27.

p. 80 **Lindsay Mills:** Paul Lewis, "Edward Snowden's Girlfriend Lindsay Mills: At the Moment I Feel Alone," *Guardian*, June 11, 2013.

4. American Amnesia

p. 83 **"Power concedes nothing without a demand":** Frederick Douglass, "West India Emancipation" speech at Canandaigua, New York, August 3, 1857.

p. 83 **"Restore the Fourth" rallies:** Rebecca Bowe, "NSA Surveillance: Protesters Stage Restore the Fourth Rallies across US," *Guardian*, July 5, 2013; Heather Kelly, "Protests against the NSA Spring Up across US," CNN, July 5, 2013.

pp. 83–4 **colorful placards:** Ben Yakas, "Photos: The 21 Best Signs from the 'Restore the Fourth' NSA Protest," *Gothamist*, July 5, 2013.

p. 84 **Reverend Billy:** "Restore the Fourth March NYC," July 5, 2013, YouTube.

p. 84 **thousands converged on Washington:** Jim Newell, "Thousands Gather in Washington for Anti-NSA 'Stop Watching Us' Rally," *Guardian*, October 26, 2013; "StopWatching.Us: Rally against Mass Surveillance 10/26/13," YouTube.

p. 84 **as if the Tea Party and Occupy Wall Street had clasped hands:** Adam Serwer, "'Stop Watching Us' Sees a Chance to Reform the NSA," MSNBC, October 26, 2013, Msnbc.com.

p. 85 **march from Union Station to the Capitol Mall:** "#StopWatchingUs Rally against Mass Surveillance: Live

Updates," *RT Question More*, October 26, 2013, rt.com.

p. 85   **Snowden statement:** Jesselyn Radack, "My Visit with Edward Snowden," *Nation*, October 17, 2013; "Stop Watching Us Rally 10/26/13 Edward Snowden Statement," YouTube.

p. 85   **"Privacy Chernobyl":** Till Wäscher, "Six Frames against Surveillance," Internet Policy Observatory, Globalnetpolicy. org .

p. 86   **eight activists broke into an FBI field office:** Betty Medsger, *The Burglary: The Discovery of J. Edgar Hoover's Secret FBI* (New York: Vintage Books, 2014).

p. 86   **headlines and televised news reports followed:** Betty Medsger, "Stolen Documents Describe FBI Surveillance Activities," *Washington Post*, March 24, 1971; Michael Isikoff, "NBC Reporter Recalls Exposing FBI Spying," NBC News, January 8, 2014.

pp. 86–7   **William Sullivan memo targeting MLK:** Tony Capaccio, "MLK's Speech Attracted FBI's Intense Attention," *Washington Post*, August 27, 2013.

p. 87   **Hoover personal letter to Sullivan:** Michael E. Ruane, "'You Are Done': A Secret Letter to Martin Luther King Jr. Sheds Light on FBI's Malice," *Washington Post*, December 13, 2017.

p. 87   **Sullivan sent King an anonymous package:** Beverly Gage, "What an Uncensored Letter to M.L.K. Reveals," *New York Times Magazine*, November 11, 2014.

pp. 87–8   **assassination of Fred Hampton:** Michael Newton, *Famous Assassinations in World History: An Encyclopedia* (ABC-CLIO, 2014), 206.

p. 88   **army had been monitoring civilians:** Richard Halloran, "Army Spied on 18,000 Civilians in 2-Year Operation," *New York Times*, January 18, 1971; Seymour M. Hersh, "Army Is Criticized on Civilian Spying," *New York Times*, August 30, 1972; John Herbers, "Senator Ervin Thinks the Constitution Should Be Taken Like Mountain Whisky—Undiluted and Untaxed," *New York Times*, November 15, 1970.

p. 88 **Watergate:** Daniel Bush, "The Complete Watergate Timeline (It Took Longer Than You Realize)," *PBS Newshour*, May 30, 2017, pbs.org.

p. 88 **Seymour Hersh scoop:** Seymour Hersh, "Huge C.I.A. Operation Reported in US against Anti-War Forces, Other Dissidents in Nixon Years," *New York Times*, December 22, 1974.

p. 89 **Church Committee:** NCC staff, "Looking Back at the Church Committee," *Constitution Daily*, National Constitution Center, January 27, 2019, Constitutioncenter. org.

p. 89 **Mondale addresses NSA director:** *Hearings before the Select Committee to Study Governmental Operations with respect to Intelligence Activities of the United States Senate*, vol. 5, *The National Security Agency and Fourth Amendment Rights, October 29 and November 6, 1975* (Washington, DC: US Government Printing Office, 1976), cryptome.org, 35–44.

pp. 89–90 **Church Committee reveals overreaching NSA programs:** Katelyn Epsley-Jones and Christina Frenzel, "The Church Committee Hearings and the FISA Court," PBS Frontline, May 15, 2007, pbs.org.

p. 90 **Cointelpro, "a sophisticated vigilante operation":** US Senate, *Final Report of the Select Committee to Study Governmental Operations with respect to Intelligence Activities*, book 3, *Supplementary Detailed Staff Reports on Intelligence Activities and the Rights of Americans* (Washington, DC: US Government Printing Office, 1976), 2.

p. 91 **Bork harrumphs:** Robert J. Bork, "'Reforming' Foreign Intelligence," *Wall Street Journal*, March 9, 1978.

p. 91 **classified opinions:** Cora Currier, Justin Elliott, and Theodoric Meyer, "Mass Surveillance in America: A Timeline of Loosening Laws and Practices," ProPublica, June 7, 2013, projects.propublica.org.

p. 91 **secret court would authorize 33,942 warrants:** Evan Perez, "Secret Court's Oversight Gets Scrutiny," *Wall Street Journal*, June 20, 2013.

p. 91 **as fires still burned in the wreckage at Ground Zero:** "Ground Zero Stops Burning, after 100 Days," *Guardian*, December 20, 2001.

pp. 91–2 **Stuart Taylor Jr.:** Stuart Taylor, "The Big Snoop: Life, Liberty, and the Pursuit of Terrorists," Brookings Institute, April 29, 2014, csweb.brookings.edu.

pp. 92–3 **Senator Church on *Meet the Press*:** "The Intelligence Gathering Debate—www.NBCUniversalArchives.com," *Meet the Press*, August 17, 1975, YouTube.

p. 93 **call for a new Church Committee:** Mark Jaycox, "Former Church Committee Staffers Tell Congress to Reassert Authority as 40th Anniversary of Church Committee Comes to Close," Electronic Frontier Foundation, October 13, 2015, Eff.org; Mark Rumold, "Former Church Committee Council and Staffers Call on Congress to Create Modern Day Church Committee," Electronic Frontier Foundation, March 17, 2014, Eff.org.

p. 93 **USA Freedom Act:** "USA Freedom Act: What's In, What's Out," *Washington Post*, June 2, 2015; Cindy Cohn and Rainey Reitman, "USA Freedom Act Passes: What We Celebrate, What We Mourn, and Where We Go From Here," Electronic Frontier Foundation, June 2, 2015, eff.org.

p. 93 **Hundreds of millions of records purged:** Charlie Savage, "N.S.A. Purges Hundreds of Millions of Call and Text Records," *New York Times*, June 28, 2018.

p. 93 **German media scholar Till Wäscher**: Wäscher, "Six Frames against Surveillance."

p. 94 **Apple CEO Tim Cook:** Eric Lichtblau and Katie Benner, "Apple Fights Order to Unlock San Bernardino Gunman's iPhone," *New York Times*, February 17, 2016; Kate Fazzini, "In a Three-Way Privacy Fight, Apple Has More to Lose Than Facebook or Google," CNBC, October 25, 2018.

p. 94 **Justice Department officials derided the company's refusal to cooperate:** Eric Lichtblau and Matt Apuzzo, "Justice Department Calls Apple's Refusal to Unlock iPhone a 'Marketing Strategy,'" *New York Times*, February 19, 2016.

p. 94 **Snowden told the *Guardian* he had no regrets:** Ewen MacAskill and Alex Hern, "Edward Snowden: The People Are Still Powerless, but Now They're Aware," *Guardian*, June 4, 2018.

p. 95 **John Oliver in Times Square:** Adam Chandler, "What It Takes to Make People Care about NSA Surveillance," *Atlantic*, April 6, 2015; "Government Surveillance: Last Week Tonight with John Oliver (HBO)," YouTube.

p. 95 **Nearly half of Americans "not very concerned":** Lee Rainie and Mary Madden, "Americans' Privacy Strategies Post-Snowden," Pew Research Center, March 16, 2015, Pewresearch.org.

p. 95 **surveillance fatigue and "so-what surveillance":** Nick Kolakowski, "The NSA and Surveillance Fatigue," *Dice*, October 15, 2013, insights.dice.com/; Kelton Sears, "Alexa and the Dawn of So-What Surveillance," *Seattle Weekly*, March 29, 2017, seattleweekly.com.

5. The Panopticon in the Parlor

p. 97 **"Everybody Knows":** Leonard Cohen, from *I'm Your Man* (CBS Records, 1988).

p. 97 **Farhad Manjoo:** Farhad Manjoo, "Why We May Soon Be Living in Alexa's World," *New York Times*, February 21, 2018.

pp. 97–8 **Twitter followers respond to Manjoo:** Matthew, twitter. com/lazarus7/status/910221860331151360; Wide Spacer, twitter.com/WideSpacer/status/910196823880544257.

p. 98 **Echo could be transformed into a wiretap:** Mark Barnes, "Alexa, Are You Listening?," F-Secure Labs, August 1, 2017, labs.mwrinfosecurity.com.

p. 98 **creepy, witch-like laughter**: Venessa Wong, "Amazon Knows Alexa Devices Are Laughing Spontaneously and It's 'Working to Fix It,'" *BuzzFeed News*, March 7, 2018, Buzzfeednews.com; "Alexa's Creepy Laughter Has Amazon Echo Users Puzzled," *Today*, NBC, March 7, 2018.

pp. 98–9 **conversation about hardwood floors:** Gary Horcher, "Woman Says Her Amazon Device Recorded Private Conversation, Sent It out to Random Contact," KIRO-7 News, Seattle, May 25, 2018, Kiro7.com.

pp. 98–9 **sinister hockey puck:** Emily Flake, "Why Is Alexa Laughing? Some Theories," *New Yorker*, March 9, 2018.

p. 99 **Amazon had sold an estimated 10.7 million Alexa-powered devices:** Nat Levy, "Amazon Passes 10M Alexa-Powered Devices Sold, Survey Says, with More Models on the Way," *GeekWire*, May 8, 2017, Geekwire.com.

p. 99 **25 million smart speakers sold:** Associated Press, "Smart Speaker Sales More than Tripled in 2017," Billboard, May 8, 2018, Billboard.com.

p. 99 **prediction: in 2020 three-quarters of American homes will have smart speakers:** "The Smart Audio Report, Spring

2019," National Public Media, Nationalpublicmedia.com.

p. 99   **number of voice-activated assistants could rival earth's human population:** Judith Shulevitz, "Alexa, Should We Trust You?," *Atlantic*, November 2018; Ronan De Renesse, "Digital Assistant and Voice AI–Capable Device Forecast: 2016–21," *Ovum*, April 28, 2017, ovum.informa.com.

p. 99   **surveillance capitalism:** Shoshona Zuboff, *The Age of Surveillance Capitalism: The Fight for a Human Future at the New Frontier of Power* (PublicAffairs, 2019).

p. 101   **Amazon technology analyzes human voice to determine ethnic origin, gender, age, health, and mental state:** Madison Malone Kircher, "I Don't Want My Echo Dot to Be Able to Tell When I'm Sick," *New York*, October 15, 2018; Belle Lin, "Amazon's Accent Recognition Technology Could Tell the Government Where You're From," *Intercept*, November 15, 2018; Jon Brodkin, "Amazon Patents Alexa Tech to Tell if You're Sick, Depressed and Sell You Meds," *Ars Technica*, October 11, 2018, arstechnica.com.

p. 102   **Cambridge Analytica:** Matthew Rosenberg, Nicholas Confessore, and Carole Cadwalladr, "How Trump Consultants Exploited the Facebook Data of Millions," *New York Times*, March 17, 2018.

p. 102   **information on as many as eighty-seven million people:** Paul Chadwick, "How Many People Had Their Data Harvested by Cambridge Analytica?" *Guardian*, April 16, 2018.

p. 102   **everyone from credit card companies to health insurers showed interest in Facebook:** Astra Taylor and Jathan Sadowski, "How Companies Turn Your Facebook Activity into a Credit Score," *Nation*, May 27, 2015; "Big Data, Financial Services and Privacy," *Economist*, February 9, 2017.

p. 102   **unearthing the Cambridge Analytica scandal:** Nicholas

Confessore, "Cambridge Analytica and Facebook: The Scandal and the Fallout So Far," *New York Times*, April 4, 2018.

p. 103   **Grindr disclosed users' HIV status:** Azeen Ghorayshi and Sri Ray, "Grindr Is Letting Other Companies See User HIV Status and Location Data," *BuzzFeed*, April 2, 2018.

p. 103   **police used an Ohio man's pacemaker data:** Ms. Smith, "Cops Use Pacemaker Data to Charge Homeowner with Arson, Insurance Fraud," *CSO*, Jan 30, 2017, csoonline.com.

p. 103   **"stingrays" that mimic mobile phone towers:** "Stingray Tracking Devices: Who's Got Them?," America Civil Liberties Union, November 2018, Aclu.org.

p. 104   **alarmed members of Congress wrote a letter to Jeff Bezos about Recognition:** Edward Markey et al., "Dear Mr. Bezos," https://t.co/k9OGVIEQ05.

p. 104   **surveillance system made up of networked doorbell cameras:** Jacob Snow, "Amazon's Disturbing Plan to Add Face Surveillance to Your Front Door," American Civil Liberties Union, December 12, 2018, Aclu.org; Matt McFarland, "Amazon May Want to Identify Burglars with Facial Recognition Tech," CNN Business, November 30, 2018, Cnn. com; Mark Frauenfelder, "Amazon Patents Doorbell Camera that Calls Police When It Recognizes a 'Suspicious' Person," *BoingBoing*, December 14, 2018, boingboing.net.

p. 104   **Bentonville, Arkansas, police:** Alfred Ng, "Police Request Echo Recordings for Homicide Investigation," CNET, December 27, 2016, Cnet.com; Tom Dotan and Reed Albergotti, "Amazon Echo and the Hot Tub Murder," *The Information*, December 27, 2016, theinformation.com.

p. 104   **New Hampshire judge ordered Amazon to release recordings:** Meagan Flynn, "Police Think Alexa May Have Witnessed a New Hampshire Double Homicide. Now They

Want Amazon to Turn Her Over," *Washington Post,* November 14, 2018.

p. 104 **Prosecutors obtained the victim's FitBit records:** Christine Hauser, "In Connecticut Murder Case, a Fitbit Is a Silent Witness," *New York Times,* April 27, 2017.

pp. 104–5 **Champlain University in Vermont:** "Internet of Things Forensics," Leahy Center for Digital Forensics and Cybersecurity, leahycenterblog.champlain.edu.

p. 105 **Alexa's random laughter:** "Alexa's Creepy Laughter Has Amazon Echo Users Puzzled," *Today,* NBC, March 7, 2018.

p. 106 **government secretly used census data to target Japanese Americans:** Lori Aratani, "Secret Use of Census Info Helped Send Japanese Americans to Internment Camps in WWII," *Washington Post,* April 6, 2018.

p. 107 **writers will censor themselves:** J. M. Coetzee, *Giving Offense: Essays on Censorship* (Chicago: University of Chicago Press, 1996), 9.

p. 107 **PEN survey:** *Chilling Effects: NSA Surveillance Drives US Writers to Self-Censor* (New York: PEN American Center, 2013), pen.org.

p. 108 **drop in online traffic to terrorism-related Wikipedia articles:** Jonathon W. Penney, "Chilling Effects: Online Surveillance and Wikipedia Use," *Berkeley Technology Law Journal* 31, no. 1 (2016), doi.org.

p. 108 **researchers noticed "chilling effects":** Alex Marthews and Catherine Tucker, "Government Surveillance and Internet Search Behavior," SSRN, dx.doi.org.

p. 108 **more internet users participating in "privacy-enhancing activities":** Sören Preibusch, "Privacy Behaviors after Snowden," *Communications of the ACM* 58, no. 5 (May 2015): 48.

p. 109 **Richards: "shadowy regimes":** Neil M. Richards, "The

Dangers of Surveillance," *Harvard Law Review* 126, no. 7 (May 20, 2013), harvardlawreview.org.

p. 109   **Edward Abbey:** Edward Abbey, *Desert Solitaire* (New York: McGraw-Hill, 1968), 129.

p. 110   **Marlinspike:** Moxie Marlinspike, "We Should All Have Something to Hide," blog post, June 12, 2013, moxie.org.

p. 110   **interracial marriage:** *Loving v. Virginia*, 388 US 1 (1967), supreme.justia.com.

p. 110   **gay marriage:** Adam Liptak, "Supreme Court Ruling Makes Same-Sex Marriage a Right Nationwide," *New York Times*, June 26, 2015.

p. 111   **arrest of smartphone-wielding citizens:** Jamiles Lartey, "Film-makers Demand Inquiry into 'Targeting' of People Who Record Police," *Guardian*, August 11, 2016.

p. 112   **"God was the original surveillance camera":** Julie Scharper, "Artist Hasan Elahi Meticulously Documents Life after FBI Investigation," *Baltimore Sun*, January 22, 2013.

p. 112   **Domestic abusers spying on spouses:** William Turton, "Abusive Partners Are Now Tracking Their Spouses with Apps Made to Watch Their Kids," *Vice*, September 16, 2018.

p. 112   **Walmart technology to spy on cashiers:** "Listening to the Frontend," US Patent 10,020,004 B2, United States Patent Office, July 10, 2018, pdfpiw.uspto.gov/.

p. 112   **Amazon patented a bracelet to track warehouse workers:** "Ultrasonic Bracelet and Receiver for Detecting Position in 2d Plane," US Patent 2017/0278051 A1, United States Patent Office, September 28, 2017, pdfaiw.uspto.gov/.

p. 112   **Stockholm startups embedding microchips under employees' skin:** Jena McGregor, "Some Swedish Workers Are Getting Microchips Implanted in Their Hands," *Washington Post*, April 4, 2017.

p. 112 **Three Square Market created a similar program:** Danielle Paquette, "Some Feared Hackers and the Devil. Others Got Microchipped," *Washington Post*, August 1, 2017.

pp. 112–13 **"internet of people" and locking workers in the bathroom:** Erik Lorenzsonn, "Wisconsin Company That Microchipped Its Workers Envisions an 'Internet of People,'" *Cap Times*, January 24, 2018.

p. 113 **Pentagon-backed research used to forecast crime:** Ali Winston and Ingrid Burrington, "A Pioneer in Predictive Policing Is Starting a Troubling New Project," *Verge*, April 26, 2018.

p. 113 **"broken windows" theory:** Sarah Childress, "The Problem with "Broken Windows" Policing," *Frontline*, June 28, 2016, pbs.org.

p. 113 **it perpetuates discrimination:** Nathan Munn, "This Predictive Policing Company Compares Its Software to 'Broken Windows' Policing," *Vice*, June 11, 2018.

p. 113 **Palantir draws protests:** Rob Copeland and Eliot Brown, "Palantir Has a $20 Billion Valuation and a Bigger Problem: It Keeps Losing Money," *Wall Street Journal*, November 12, 2018.

p. 113 **Xinjiang province:** "China: Minority Region Collects DNA from Millions, Private Information Gathered by Police, under Guise of Public Health Program," Human Rights Watch, December 13, 2017, hrw.org.

p. 113 **Hangzhou:** "Beijing to Judge Every Resident Based on Behavior by End of 2020," *Bloomberg News,* November 21, 2018.

p. 113 **Goal: paralyzing "untrustworthy" people:** ibid.

6. The Tree

p. 124 **Jeremy Scahill told the audience:** Emily Buder, "Why Laura Poitras Is the 'Most Badass Female Filmmaker' and More from 'CITIZENFOUR' NYFF Premiere," *IndieWire*, October 11, 2014, indiewire.com.

p. 124 **Lonnie Snowden:** Debbi Wilgoren, "Snowden's Father on 'Today': He Betrayed His Government, but He's Not a Traitor," *Washington Post*, June 28, 2013.

p. 125 **an entire federal office processing FOIA rejections:** Julia Barton, "Neither Confirm nor Deny," *Radio Lab*, June 4, 2019, wnycstudios.org.

p. 128 **First Look CEO Michael Bloom's letter to staff:** Maxwell Tani, "The Intercept Shuts Down Access to Snowden Trove, *Daily Beast*, March 14, 2019, thedailybeast.com.

p. 128 **Laura Poitras's letter to the board of directors:** Barrett Brown, "Why the Intercept Really Closed the Snowden Archive," *Medium*, March 27, 2019, medium.com.

p. 128 **Laura Poitras barred from attending meeting:** Maxwell Tani, "The Intercept Bars Co-Founder from Meeting after Snowden Archive Shutdown," *Daily Beast*, March 14, 2019, thedailybeast.com.

p. 129 **Rumors spread that the company was buying Passionflix:** Sarah Jones, "Tensions Rise at First Look Media as Company Shifts Strategy," *New York Magazine*, July 17, 2019, nymag. com.

p. 129 **"barometer of naughtiness":** Passionflix, Passionflix.com/ bon.

p. 129 **Passionflix acquisition finalized:** "First Look Media, Passionflix Strike Streaming Partnership," MSNBC, Sept. 12, 2019, YouTube.

p. 129 **Julian Assange eighteen-count indictment:** "WikiLeaks Founder Julian Assange Charged in 18-Count Superseding Indictment," US Department of Justice, May 23, 2019, justice. gov.

p. 130 **Jabber singled out in Assange indictment:** Glenn Greenwald and Micah Lee, "The US Government's Indictment of Julian Assange Poses Grave Threats to Press Freedom," *Intercept*, April 11, 2019.

p. 130 **Micah Lee comments on Assange indictment:** twitter. com/micahflee/status/1116340396643082240?lang=en.

p. 130 **Snowden comments on Assange indictment:** twitter. com/snowden/status/1131657973745496066?lang=en.

p. 131 **Snowden on humans as "pattern-recognition machines":** Poitras, *Astro Noise*, 121.

pp. 132–3 **Orwell on being human:** George Orwell, "In Front of Your Nose," *Tribune* (London), March 22, 1946.

Appendix

p. 136 **Signal's 400 percent jump in downloads**: Jeff John Roberts, "This Messaging App Saw a Surge after Trump's Election," *Fortune,* December 2, 2016.

p. 136 **Moxie Marlinspike on Trump**: Brian X. Chen, "Worried about the Privacy of Your Messages? Download Signal," *New York Times*, December 7, 2016.

p. 136 **Facebook buys WhatsApp:** Adrian Covert, "Facebook Buys WhatsApp for $19 Billion," *CNN Business*, February 19, 2014.

p. 138 **snail mail:** Scott Shane and Sarah Kliff, "A Scoop about Neil Armstrong Arrived in a Plain Brown Envelope," *New York*

Times, August 1, 2019.

p. 139 **NSA cracks VPNs:** "NSA Broke into Secure Network of Al Jazeera and Others: Report," *Al Jazeera*, August 16, 2018.

p. 140 **laptop cameras:** Katie Rogers, "Mark Zuckerberg Covers His Laptop Camera. You Should Consider It, Too," *New York Times*, June 22, 2016.

p. 140 **Little Snitch:** "Little Snitch 4," Objective Development, https://www.obdev.at/products/littlesnitch/index.html.

p. 140 **cute stickers:** Electronic Frontier Foundation, eff.org.

p. 142 **Mobile Justice:** "ACLU Apps to Record Police Conduct," Aclu.org.

p. 142 **HyperFace:** "HyperFace," Adam Harvey, ahprojects.com/hyperface.

p. 142 **CV Dazzle**: CV Dazzle, Adam Harvey, cvdazzle.com.

pp. 142–3 **Kate Bertash**: Adversarial Fashion, adversarialfashion.com.

p. 143 **EPIC guide privacy tools:** "EPIC Online Guide to Practical Privacy Tools," Electronic Privacy Information Center, Epic.org.

p. 143 **General Data Protection Regulation:** Adam Satariano, "What the G.D.P.R., Europe's Tough New Data Law, Means for You," *New York Times*, May 16, 2018.

p. 143 **California passed a law:** Daisuke Wakabayashi, "California Passes Sweeping Law to Protect Online Privacy," *New York Times*, June 28, 2018.

p. 144 **Privacy International:** "Why We've Filed Complaints against Companies that Most People Have Never Heard of — and What Needs to Happen Next," Privacy International, web.archive.org.

p. 144 **Amnesty International ranking of tech companies:** "Amnesty Int'ls Digital Privacy Assessment on 11 Companies'

Messaging Apps Ranks Facebook and Apple Top and Tencent Last," Business and Human Rights Resource Centre, Business-humanrights.org.

p. 145 **anti-gay witch hunt**: "The Egyptian Government," All Out, https://go.allout.org/en/a/egypt.

p. 145 **Color of Change:** George Joseph and Murtaza Hussain, "FBI Tracked an Activist Involved with Black Lives Matter as They Travelled across the US, Documents Show," *Intercept*, March 19, 2018.

pp. 145–6 **ACLU and doorbell cameras:** Jacob Snow, "Amazon's Disturbing Plan to Add Face Surveillance to Your Front Door," ACLU, December 12, 2018.

p. 146 **Natasha Singer:** Natasha Singer, "The Government Protects Our Food and Cars. Why Not Our Data?," *New York Times*, November 2, 2019.

Index